Bracing for the Storm
A West Florida Hurricane Survival Guide

by Brock Kingsley

Formatted, Converted, and Distributed by eBookIt.com
http://www.eBookIt.com

ISBN-13: 9781456642044 (paperback)
ISBN-13: 9781456642037 (ebook)
ISBN-13: 9781456642051 (audiobook)

Dear Esteemed Reader,

Thank you immensely for choosing this book to join your collection. We imagine that you've already embarked on an exploration of ideas within these pages, and we couldn't be happier about it!

Now, if you find yourself chuckling, pondering, or even debating with the words in front of you, we'd absolutely love to hear about it. If you can spare a few moments to pen down your thoughts in a review, we would be as delighted as a dictionary on a spelling bee!

An Amazon review would be excellent - but hey, we're far from picky. Whether it's a scribble on the back of a grocery list, a tweet, or even a message in a bottle (though that might take a while to reach us), your feedback is gold.

Writing a review might not be as fun as a spontaneous dance-off, but we promise it'll bring grins to our faces, warmth to our hearts, and incredibly valuable insights to future readers.

With Gratitude,

Bo Bennett, PhD
Publisher
Archieboy Holdings, LLC.

Table of Contents

Foreword 7

Introduction 8

   Understanding the Risk: West Florida's Hurricane History 8

   Who Should Read This Guide? 11

   How to Use This Book...13

Chapter 1: The Basics of Hurricanes..15

   What is a Hurricane? 15

   The Anatomy of a Hurricane 18

   The Hurricane Season...21

   Hurricane Categories and What They Mean...........................24

Chapter 2: Preparing Before the Season 27

   Assessing Your Risk...27

   Home Inspections and Modifications.......................................28

   Windows and Shutters 31

   Shutters 31

   Roof and Structural Integrity 33

   Stocking Emergency Supplies 35

   Food and Water 37

   First Aid Kit 39

   Power and Light Sources 41

Chapter 3: Evacuation Strategies 43

   Developing an Evacuation Plan 43

   Choosing an Evacuation Route 46

   Preparing an Evacuation Kit 48

   Pet Evacuation: Don't Forget Fluffy! 50

Chapter 4: Riding Out the Storm 52

When to Stay and When to Go 53

Safe Rooms and Shelters 55

Utility Safety: Gas, Water, and Electricity..........................57

How to Keep Informed 59

Chapter 5: Communications..62

Setting Up a Communication Plan..62

Useful Apps and Websites 65

Emergency Numbers and Contacts 67

Chapter 6: Financial and Legal Preparedness 70

Understanding Your Insurance..70

Important Documents to Protect 73

Creating a Financial Emergency Kit.....................................75

Chapter 7: Community Resources...78

Local Emergency Services 78

Community Support and Neighborhood Plans......................81

Volunteer Opportunities 84

Chapter 8: Special Considerations..88

Families with Children 88

Senior Citizens and Disabled Individuals.............................91

Care for Pets and Livestock 94

Chapter 9: Post-Storm Recovery 97

Assessing Damage Safely..97

Contacting Insurance and Authorities.................................100

Cleanup and Rebuilding 103

Coping with Psychological Effects..105

Chapter 10: Lessons from the Past...108

Case Studies: West Florida Hurricanes 108

Lessons Learned and Future Outlook 111

Appendix A: Emergency Supplies Checklist 115

Appendix B: Evacuation Route Maps 118

Appendix C: Important Contact Information 121

Foreword

As you delve into the pages of this book, the aim is to subtly reset your perspectives and attitudes toward the ever-complex world of politics. It's a topic that's often viewed in only black and white. However, this book caters to unveil the breathtaking array of grays that blanket this myriad subject.

Introduction

Living on the scenic West Coast of Florida has its benefits, with sunny skies, balmy breezes, and picturesque settings aplenty. Yet, every paradise has its snag, and in this case, it is the potentially devastating impact of the hurricane season. With a history of storm surges that have tested even the hardiest among us, the urgent need for hurricane preparedness can't be stressed enough. This book is meant to provide a comprehensive yet easy-to-follow guide to understanding hurricanes, preparing for them, weathering the storm, and recovering post-event. Drawing from historic examples while focusing on practical measures, this guide aims to turn you into an informed and prepared individual capable of facing one of nature's fiercer forces head-on. Consider it your personal trail map navigating the turbulent terrains of hurricane survival, so not only can you withstand the storm, but also bounce back in its aftermath.

Understanding the Risk: West Florida's Hurricane History

The shimmering coast of West Florida, known for its picturesque beaches, vibrant cultural scene, and irresistible weather, also serves as a constant reminder of nature's unruly power due to its recurrent hurricanes. To truly prepare for hurricanes, an understanding of the area's hurricane history is vital.

The region has a long, tumultuous timeline of hurricanes since records started. Over several decades, it has endured intense, destructive storms, with some standing out for their extraordinary power and impact.

One of the most notable hurricanes was the Okeechobee hurricane of 1928. It was a notorious category 4 storm, bringing relentless rain and robust winds causing excessive flooding and extensive damage across the area. It was a cruel reminder that Florida's beauty comes paired with a price tag of potential devastation.

Then there was Hurricane Donna in 1960. This category 4 storm was one of the most intense and long-lived hurricanes ever recorded in the Atlantic Basin, moving across Central Florida with wind speeds reaching a staggering 145 mph. The hurricane caused a great deal of destruction, highlighting the need for better preventive measures and disaster management planning.

A decade later, in 1972, Hurricane Agnes, though only a category 1 storm, brought unrelenting rainfall that affected areas across Florida to Virginia, causing severe water damage and flooding. It showcased that even a category 1 storm could cause major problems if it hangs around long enough.

In 2004, the super-active hurricane season saw four named storms hit the Florida coast in short succession. Hurricanes Charley, Frances, Ivan, and Jeanne left a trail of destruction, damaging homes and uprooting communities. The situation underpinned the need for continuous hurricane preparedness, regardless of how tranquil the skies may seem.

Hurricane Wilma in 2005 still brings shudders to the residents who experienced its wrath. The storm ripped through the Gulf coast of Florida with unexpected intensity and caused extensive damage. Wilma reiterated the weather's unpredictable nature, emphasizing the importance of always being prepared.

More recently, Hurricane Irma in 2017, a category 4 storm, showed us again that even the most modern infrastructure isn't hurricane-proof. Its destructive pathway through Florida was a grim reminder that we can't afford to ignore the looming threat of hurricanes each year.

Not to be left out in the discussion, Hurricane Michael, a category 5 storm in 2018, was a cruel reality check. It was the strongest storm on record to hit the Florida Panhandle, with wind speeds reaching a hair-raising 160mph. Michael changed the landscape, quite literally, and marked itself as a historic hurricane for the area.

The lesson? Hurricanes are a part of life for residents of West Florida. Some years are calm, while other years present more dangerous and numerous storms. Still, one thing's certain: tropical storms and hurricanes won't cease visiting this part of the state.

An insight into West Florida's hurricane history provides us a crucial context for understanding our risks and preparing accordingly. The past offers valuable lessons on the enormous power of these storms and the destruction they can wreak on homes, towns, and communities.

The takeaway is this: Preparation is king. Irrespectively of a storm's projected strength or path, having a plan and being prepared can and does save lives. Our hope is that the weather's kind to us, but we also need to respect the fact that we live in an area where hurricanes are part of the scenery.

As we delve further into this guide, we'll cover everything you need to know about getting ready for hurricane season, from understanding hurricanes and their categories to making home modifications, setting evacuation strategies, and post-storm recovery. This is your roadmap to combating hurricanes and ensuring the safety of yourself, your family, and your community.

You've now taken the first crucial step towards hurricane preparedness – gaining knowledge. Thanks for choosing to educate, empower, and prepare yourself. The journey towards safety starts here, and it starts now. We can't prevent hurricanes from hitting our beautiful coast, but together, we can lessen their impact by being prepared.

Who Should Read This Guide?

Simply put, anyone who calls the west coast of Florida home should definitely take the time to read and understand the content of this guide. Whether you're a recent transplant, have been living here in the sunny state for decades, or you're just visiting and got caught in the wrong season, this guide will provide you with essential information you need to know before, during, and after a hurricane.

You may be a young student living alone, or a senior resident living in a retirement community, the information herein is aimed at ensuring your safety regardless of age or physical ability. In fact, we have made specific considerations for families with children, senior citizens, and disabled individuals, making it a comprehensive guide for all demographic groups.

It's not just for homeowners either. Renters, landlords, property managers, everyone can benefit from the information found in these pages. From assessing the structural integrity of dwelling places to arranging for advanced precautionary measures, you'll find actionable insights tailored for everyone's unique needs.

If you have pets or livestock, this guide will serve as an important and invaluable resource. We understand that our four-legged companions and livestock are an integral part of many families and businesses on the west coast of Florida, and specific tips and strategies have been outlined to ensure their safety during hurricane events.

First-time residents and visitors to West Florida can especially benefit from this guide. The region has its unique meteorological patterns and navigating through hurricane season can be daunting when you're not familiar with the area or the seasonal cycle. This guide will give you a solid understanding of the basics of hurricanes and the best strategies to cope with them in this region.

Community leaders and volunteer emergency responders would find the information in this book quite helpful. The guide provides detailed information about local community resources, volunteer opportunities, and the templates for creating neighborhood plans for hurricane preparedness.

Perhaps you're the type who likes to be prepared for the worst-case scenario, a true survivor at heart. This guide is your ticket to being that all-important beacon of hope and knowledge when the storm hits. With details on everything from how to set up a communication plan to creating a financial emergency kit, this guide aims to turn you into a hurricane readiness guru.

This guide is also for those people who have already experienced a hurricane and think they know it all. The truth is, every hurricane is different, and being complacent can be dangerous. The latest information contained within this guide can offer you new approaches and reinforce other key safety habits that might have gotten rusty.

In summary, this guide is for anyone who is part of the vibrant, diverse west coast of Florida community. Hurricanes unfortunately are part of our reality. With this guide, we hope to make every Floridian feel empowered and more importantly, safe, when the next hurricane season rolls around.

How to Use This Book

Alright, so you've got this guide in your hands, and you're wondering how to get the most out of it. It's simple, really. Start by familiarizing yourself with the different sections of the book. Each chapter targets a specific aspect of hurricane preparedness, during and after the event. These insights are aimed to help you, the residents of the west coast of Florida, prepare for the hurricane season and ensure safety for all ages.

The book starts with fundamental knowledge about hurricanes - how they're formed, the anatomy of a hurricane, and different categories. This elementary info is in "The Basics of Hurricanes". It's not a bad idea to get your feet wet with that before diving deeper, especially if hurricanes are new territory.

Next, "Preparing Before the Season" is absolutely essential. In this section, you'll learn about home inspections, stockpiling emergency supplies, and other definitive safety measures. We'll be frank - this information can save lives. So, treat it with importance and you'll be well on your way.

God forbid you'd have to evacuate, but being prepared for this scenario is better than being caught off guard. You'll find details about evacuation plans, routes, and how to keep Fluffy the cat safe in "Evacuation Strategies".

If you decide to stay put during the storm, check out "Riding Out the Storm". It teaches you about identifying safe places in your home and maintaining utility safety. Also, keeping informed during a hurricane can't be stressed enough, and you'll find ways of doing so here.

Naturally, having a rock solid communication plan in place is crucial. "Communications", covers that ground. We'll guide you through setting up a plan and various apps and websites that could prove invaluable.

There's also an entire section dedicated to "Financial and Legal Preparedness". Going through this is like doing your homework before the big test. It allows you to understand the ins and outs of insurance, protecting important documents, and prepping a financial emergency kit.

Community resources and neighborhood plans can create the collective safety net that we all need in times of distress. Find this information in "Community Resources". And then, there are "Special Considerations". This is more like a guide within the guide, catering to families with children, senior citizens, people with disabilities, and even pets and livestock.

We couldn't leave out the inevitable aftermath, could we? So, "Post-Storm Recovery" is all about assessing damage, contacting authorities, cleanup, rebuilding, and psychological support.

Wrapping up, "Lessons from the Past" gives you tales of West Florida Hurricanes - what we learned and our future outlook with regards to hurricanes. Toward the end, the appendices have some handy checklists, contact information, and route maps that you can directly refer to for quick checks.

Chapter 1: The Basics of Hurricanes

Easing into the nitty-gritty of hurricanes, let's start with the fundamentals. You're probably asking, what on Earth is a hurricane exactly? Well, at its core, a hurricane is a massive, swirling storm that forms over warm waters in tropical areas. They pack quite a punch with winds that typically rev up to a whopping 74 mph or higher. But wait, there's more! Besides gusty winds, hurricanes bring along heavy rainfall, storm surges, and sometimes, they even whip up tornadoes. It's like they're throwing a destructive party, and trust us, it's one fiesta you don't want to crash. But when do these tempestuous parties mostly occur? That would be during hurricane season, which traditionally runs from June 1st through November 30th. Yeah, half the year, every year! Now, not all hurricanes are created equal. They're actually rated on a scale of 1 to 5, known as categories, based on wind speed. Category 1 being a bit rough, like a wild rollercoaster ride, and category 5, being a full-throttle, hold onto your hats, thrill ride. Each category possesses its own unique threats and requires slightly different preparation and response, but don't fret, we'll cover all that in the coming chapters. So, with the basics under your belt, you're now ready to navigate this winding path to becoming a bona fide hurricane guru.

What is a Hurricane?

So, what exactly is a hurricane? To put it simply, a hurricane is a severe weather system that forms over warm ocean waters near the equator. They're essentially giant engines powered by what may seem strange: warm moist air. This air rises, creating low pressure beneath it. Higher pressure air then rushes in, becoming warm and moist in turn, and starts the cycle anew.

This constant cycle of air creates an upward spiral, with thunderstorms forming as the warm air climbs and cools. As these thunderstorms become stronger and more frequent, they can combine, forming a circular pattern of storm clouds – this is what we'd call a tropical storm.

And when conditions are right – particularly when the ocean's surface temperature is above 78 degrees Fahrenheit or so – these tropical storms can grow in size and intensity becoming hurricanes. Right, let's dive in a little bit more.

The term 'hurricane' comes from the Carib word, 'Huracan'. Funny enough, Huracan was a god of evil in their mythology. Hurricanes are famous (or should I say infamous) for their strong winds, heavy rain, and the massive ocean waves they can trigger, called storm surges.

Due to Earth's rotation, the trajectory of hurricanes in the Northern Hemisphere is typically from east to west - this is why we in Florida often like to keep an eye on the weather reports in Africa! In the Southern Hemisphere, it's a different story, with hurricanes generally moving from west to east.

Actually, did you know that depending on where they take place, hurricanes can be referred to by different names? Yeah, that's right – the same type of storm is called a 'typhoon' in the western Pacific Ocean and a 'cyclone' in the Indian Ocean and South Pacific. Nonetheless, they're all the same thing - immensely powerful and potentially dangerous storms.

In the West Florida context, hurricanes are a regular part of life, part of our unique natural characteristics, if you will. But, just because hurricanes happen often doesn't mean they're not dangerous. Quite the opposite: hurricanes can cause significant damage or even claim lives if people aren't prepared. So, learning about them is key to staying safe.

One way that meteorologists measure a hurricane's power is by its wind speed. In the United States, we use the Saffir-Simpson scale, which takes into account the hurricane's sustained wind speed and categorizes the hurricane from category 1 to 5. Category 5 hurricanes are the strongest, with wind speeds above 156 miles per hour.

But hurricanes aren't just wind. No siree, they bring along a whole heap of other weather phenomena, too. Aside from the aforementioned storm surge, hurricanes can also drop torrential rainfall causing flooding, and they can even spawn tornadoes. You may be thinking, "Wow, hurricanes sound intense," and they sure are, but there's also something fascinating about them too.

A hurricane's formation and life cycle are complex, involving a combination of precise climatological conditions. While thoroughly understanding these intricacies isn't necessary for preparing for a hurricane, it's quite the tale of nature's power and complexity.

Here's something neat: a hurricane is organized into distinct parts. Those heavy clouds and rain spiraling outwards? Those are the rainbands. The calm, clear, eye in the middle? Yep, that's the hurricane's eye. The worst winds, rain, and storm surge? You'll find those in the eyewall. We'll be exploring all the parts and their role in a hurricane later in "The Anatomy of a Hurricane".

What's more, the effects of a hurricane can reach far beyond its immediate location. Storm systems can create rip currents and high seas hundreds of miles from a hurricane's center. Sometimes, they can even impact the weather across continents. That's how potent these storms can be!

Now, don't worry, we won't leave you just knowing all these threats without a plan! Over the course of this book, we'll delve into these topics and guide you step-by-step in crafting your own personal hurricane preparedness strategy. One thing's for sure, a hurricane is a force to be respected, and being equipped with knowledge and a plan is your best defense.

In the next section, we'll start to pull apart this weather beast and look at its different parts. Knowing the anatomy of a hurricane will not only increase your understanding of these weather monsters, but will also help you understand the reports on the television, radio, or Internet. So stay tuned, as we continue our tropical storm exploration. It's an exciting journey; we're glad you're along for the ride!

The Anatomy of a Hurricane

A hurricane, while a destructive force of nature, can also be seen as an amazing feat of atmospheric science. Understanding its structure or anatomy can help us grasp the different stages of a hurricane and a forecast's implications.

At the very core of a hurricane is what's known as the eye. Contrary to what you might expect, it's surprisingly serene in the eye. We're talking clear skies, slight winds - it's a real calm section of the storm. This can be deceptive, though. It's important to remember that the eye's formation signifies a maturing, strengthening storm.

The eye is typically an almost perfectly circular area, 20 to 40 miles wide. Its peaceful nature is surrounded by the eye wall - a towering ring of thunderstorms. The strongest winds and most severe weather conditions in a hurricane are typically found within the eye wall.

Moving away from the central eye and eye wall, we encounter rain bands. These are spiraling arms of rain and thunderstorms, often extending hundreds of miles from the hurricane's center. They deliver the storm surges, heavy rains, and gusty winds that can cause flooding and damage even in places not directly hit by the eye.

Above these components soars the hurricane's home, the upper-level outflow. Here, the top layer of the hurricane expels air, shaping an anvil-like 'canopy' over the storm that helps perpetuate its life cycle.

Now, you can't talk about hurricane anatomy without discussing its fuel source: warm, moist air from ocean surfaces. When water evaporates, it rises until it cools and transforms into cloud droplets, releasing heat in the process. This heat powers the hurricane, drawing in more air and moisture from the ocean's surface and fueling sustained wind speeds above 74 mph.

A hurricane doesn't exist in a vacuum, either. It's influenced by surrounding atmospheric and ocean conditions. Dry air can dehydrate a hurricane, while wind shear – changes in wind speed and direction with height - can tear it apart. Cooler sea temperatures can essentially starve a hurricane of its energy source.

It's fascinating, yet terrifying, knowing how each component of a hurricane interacts to create such a fierce storm system. Understanding these structures is crucial. It helps scientists predict the intensity and path of a hurricane, allowing communities time to prepare.

Our West Florida communities have weathered hurricanes before, each holding stories of the eyes passing overhead with their eerie calm, then the explosive punch of the eye wall. As residents of such an area, having appreciation for the raw power and intricate anatomy of these storms has practical implications.

During hurricane season, when a storm bears down on your community, you'll hear forecasters talk about the eye's potential path – that's their best guess as to where the strongest part of the storm will hit. They'll also talk about the risk of storm surge, which is driven by the hurricane's intense winds and low pressure. In short, understanding the anatomy of a hurricane helps you comprehend not just the danger of these storms but also the safety steps you ought to take.

When the time comes to prepare or evacuate for a storm, a clear understanding of hurricane components - the eye, eye wall, rain bands, and upper-level outflow - can help you interpret forecasts, separating the highest risk areas from safer zones. And when the sky opens up with serene calm amid the storm, you might recognize the eye's passage and brace for the following fury of the eye wall.

The hurricane's anatomy isn't uniform, either. Sometimes, the hurricane's structure will change, its eyewall will 'breathe' in a process called an eyewall replacement cycle, occasionally resulting in a temporary weakening phase, but eventually leading to a larger, potentially more destructive storm.

The anatomy of a hurricane is a testament to the wild and unpredictable nature of our planet. And while it's a fascinating object of study, remember that what you learn here isn't just academic; it's practical knowledge that is essential for survival during Florida's inevitable hurricane seasons.

Ultimately, understanding how hurricanes work will aid in understanding the risks they pose and how to prepare for them, making you better equipped to protect yourself and your loved ones.

The Hurricane Season

If there's one thing every resident on the West Coast of Florida knows, it's that there's a distinct change in the atmosphere that marks the beginning of the hurricane season. It's nearly palpable. If you were to summarize Florida's weather, you'd probably say that it's pretty much summer year-round, peppered with daily afternoon thunderstorms and occasional cold spells. But it's not that simple when it comes to hurricanes.

The official hurricane season stretches from June 1st to November 30th, with a peak typically occurring between August and October. However, hurricanes aren't beholden to calendars. The dominant forces that steer these storms' paths involve a complex dance between ocean temperatures, atmospheric conditions, and even dust blowing in from across the Atlantic.

No two hurricane seasons are ever the same. Some years are quiet, with a handful of storms stirring up the ocean without ever making landfall. Other years, Florida takes multiple hits or narrowly avoids a major catastrophe. The unpredictability of the hurricane season keeps weather experts on their toes, but it also makes it essential for residents to stay prepared especially anyone calling West Florida home.

Each season's intensity is influenced by large-scale climate patterns, including El Niño and La Niña which, in simplest terms, are characterized by the warming or cooling of the ocean in the equatorial Pacific. If you're wondering how a storm off South America's western coast impacts a hurricane forming off Africa, you wouldn't be alone. But weather systems are interconnected. An El Niño event thousands of miles away suppresses hurricane activity in the Atlantic basin.

Another significant factor in hurricane formation is the sea surface temperature. Hurricanes are fueled by heat, which they draw from the warm oceans. As ocean temperatures rise due to climate change, the potential for stronger hurricanes also increases. The summer months are especially conducive since the water temperatures in the tropics rise above the critical threshold necessary for hurricane development.

Meander over to the island of Saharan Africa. It's fascinating to think that a dust storm in the Saharan desert could alter the course or even inhibit the formation of a hurricane over the Atlantic. But it does. Tropical cyclones struggle to form or intensify in the presence of dry, dusty air. Hence, when the Saharan Air Layer migrates over the Atlantic, like clockwork, during the summertime, its propensity to create unfavorable conditions for hurricane growth is noted.

Florida, more than any other state, bears the brunt of the Atlantic hurricane season. Located on a peninsula between the warm currents of the Atlantic Ocean and the Gulf of Mexico, the Sunshine State is a prime target for hurricanes and tropical storms. It acts like a U-turn sign in terms of steering the path of storms northward.

Even if a hurricane doesn't make landfall, the effects can still reach Florida's West Coast. Tropical systems can generate significant storm surges, triggering flooding in coastal and low-lying areas. Let's not forget about the high winds - these can reach far and wide, tearing down power lines, uprooting trees, and damaging homes. And then there's the incessant rainfall, which can flood rivers and create dangerous flash flooding.

When a hurricane makes its way onto land, its intensity usually drops as it loses its source of energy: warm ocean water. However, as recent years have shown, hurricanes can maintain their intensity or even increase it as they cross over the warm, shallow waters off Florida's West Coast. This phenomenon, known as 'Brown Ocean Effect,' means that even a tropical depression or tropical storm can pack more punch than residents might expect.

Each hurricane season in Florida offers a different story. It serves up a mixed bag of storms ranging from benign, brush-by systems to catastrophic, direct-hit hurricanes. Learning to understand and respect these powerful forces of nature is key to surviving storm season in the Sunshine State.

Scientists and meteorologists utilize a myriad of tools to track these storms as they form. From advanced weather satellites in space to the brave hurricane hunters that fly directly into these tempests, we now have a better understanding of hurricanes than ever before. But remember, their job is to issue the warnings—it is our responsibility to heed them.

So when the wind shifts and the palms rustle a little harder, it's a reminder that it's time to prepare, pay attention, and always respect the power of the storm. Hurricane season is an inevitable chapter in the annals of Florida life and history.

The more we understand it, the better we can navigate it. Keep this in mind as we dive next into the distinctions and meaning of hurricane categories.

Hurricane Categories and What They Mean

The importance of understanding hurricane categories can't be overstated. It helps us predict the potential destruction and damage in case a hurricane hits. To help make this information more accessible, the Saffir-Simpson Hurricane Wind Scale was established. This scale breaks down hurricanes into five distinct classifications known as categories.

Each category is defined by the wind speeds the storm produces. Hurricanes don't just involve powerful wind gusts, though. They are also associated with storm surge, heavy rainfall, and flooding, which can cause a lot of destruction. However, the scale primarily focuses on wind speed as it's a consistent measure of the hurricane's strength.

Here's a breakdown explaining what each category represents:

Category 1:

In this first stage, wind speeds range from 74 to 95 mph. Elevated water levels with dangerous waves can lead to coastal road flooding and minor pier damage. Damage to building structures is generally restricted to roofing material, gutter systems, and unsecured lightweight objects being blown about. Unprotected windows may experience damage and extensive power outages are possible.

Category 2:

The winds in a Category 2 hurricane range from 96 to 110 mph. Here, there is potential for major damage to roofing and siding materials, as well as uprooting trees, which could block roads and damage power lines, leading to power loss potentially lasting several days.

Category 3:

Here, winds range from 111 to 129 mph. This is the first category that signifies major hurricanes, which bring devastating damage. Buildings may suffer structural damage, and electricity and water supply could be out for several days to weeks afterward.

Category 4:

Wind speeds increase to a range of 130 to 156 mph in Category 4 storms. Catastrophic damage is expected, meaning severe damage to building structures, and trees and power poles can be uprooted, isolating residential areas. The territory hit by this hurricane will be uninhabitable for weeks or months.

Category 5:

The top category, with wind speeds of 157 mph or more, signifies a hurricane of terrifying power. A high percentage of framed homes will be destroyed, with total roof failure and collapsing walls. Power outages will last for weeks to possibly months, and most of the area hit will be uninhabitable for weeks or months.

These descriptions and categories, give residents an impression of the power and potential danger posed by a storm. However, it's important to note that even lower category hurricanes can cause serious damage and should be taken seriously.

Being located on the hurricane-prone west coast of Florida, understanding hurricane categories and what they entail is crucial to effective preparation. Even a Category 1 hurricane can have serious implications. That's why we can't afford to be complacent when it comes to hurricane season.

The point of understanding all this is not to create an environment of fear or anxiety, but to promote awareness and preparedness. When we understand what we're up against, we can act accordingly by making necessary preparations.

Remember, your safety is top priority. Knowing what each hurricane category means and how much destruction each one could cause enables you to make judicious decisions regarding staying put or heeding evacuation orders. It also helps you prepare your home and yourself for the storm's potential impact, optimizing your chances of coming out of it in the best shape possible.

Ultimately, understanding hurricanes and their categories is vital for anyone living in hurricane-prone locations like the Florida west coast. It gives us a way to gauge the potential danger and make sure we're ready. This knowledge could very well be the difference between life and death when a hurricane strikes.

Chapter 2: Preparing Before the Season

Now that we've grasped a basic understanding of hurricanes and what they can do, let's talk about how to prepare for them before the season even starts. Your first task should be to assess your risk. What's the hurricane history like in your specific area? Does your home sit in a flood zone? These are critical questions to find answers to. It's also a good idea to get a thorough home inspection. Trained professionals can help you determine whether your windows, shutters, roof, and overall structure can withstand a hurricane and suggest any necessary modifications. Remember that prevention is less costly and less stressful than dealing with the aftermath of a damaged home. Additionally, get your emergency supplies ready, keeping in mind things like non-perishable food, water, first aid kits, and essential power and lighting options. Think ahead, be proactive, and you're halfway there in terms of hurricane preparedness.

Assessing Your Risk

Assessing your personal risk is crucial when it comes to hurricane preparedness. Just because you're in Florida doesn't mean you're necessarily staring down eminent catastrophe. Your risk might greatly vary depending on where you live, the structure of your home, and several other factors.

First off, take a good look at your location. Are you in a coastal area or situated further inland? Living near the water might promise great views and plenty of salty breezes, but it also means a higher risk when hurricanes are on the horizon. Areas that sit at a lower elevation or are closer to sea level might be more prone to dangerous storm surges.

Next, consider your home itself. Is it an older structure, or was it recently built to modern building codes? A house constructed pre-2002 (before Florida introduced more rigorous hurricane protection standards in building codes) likely has an increased risk compared to a house that's built to withstand extreme winds. You also need to take into account if the surrounding vegetation and trees pose a potential hazard. Even if you're not directly on the coast, strong winds can turn tree branches into hurtling projectiles. Lastly, find out if you're in a flood zone. When a hurricane barrels through, it's not just wind you need to worry about, but also heavy rains and the potential for flooding. Understanding these factors will go a long way in providing clarity on the level of risk you personally face and the most effective strategies for preparation.

Home Inspections and Modifications

Our home is our haven where we seek shelter, security, and warmth. So, when you're up against the destructive force of a hurricane, making sure your home can stand strong is critical. Home inspections and modifications are tangible steps to ensure your safety and minimize damage.

Start with a thorough inspection of your home. If you're not a DIYer, have a professional conduct a comprehensive audit. This will help identify weak spots and areas that may need attention or reinforcement.

Let's start with the foundation. Check for cracks in your slab or crawl space, as hurricanes can cause severely damaging floods. If you spot any cracks, it's crucial to fix them before hurricane season rolls around. Hurricane-force winds can exacerbate these cracks, leading to significant structural damage.

Next, check out your doors. All exterior doors, including garage doors, should have at least three hinges and a deadbolt lock that is an inch long minimum. Take into consideration that wind pressures during a hurricane can affect different parts of the house differently. You might want to reinforce your doors by adding braces or even replace them with more robust, hurricane-rated ones.

Another crucial structure to survey is your roof. Your roof is the first line of defense against heavy rains and winds. Look for loose or missing shingles, cracks, or signs of wear or decay. Pay extra attention to your roof covering and ensure it's secured to the roof deck. If you have any gables, make sure they're adequately braced to reduce wind pressure.

Check your attic ventilation points too. Winds can enter and cause an upward pressure leading to roof failure. Install a gable end bracing, and reinforce the connections of your roof to wall framing system. Always remember, it's the small things that can make a big difference.

It's a great idea to strengthen your connections. For example, connecting your roof to walls can help the building envelope hold up the violent winds. Using metal connectors and wraps can substantially improve your home's resistance to high winds.

The story doesn't end there. You need to survey your landscape too. Trim overhanging branches from trees that are too close to your house to prevent them from causing damage. Furthermore, rocks and gravel can break windows during a storm; consider replacing them with shredded bark or other soft materials.

Another major consideration is your home's proximity to water bodies. If you live near a beach or river, consider building a flood barrier. This could be something as simple as a sandbag wall or something more permanent like a raised earth levee or a concrete wall.

Check your systems as well. Make sure your electrical system components, including the circuits and switches, are raised above your home's flood level. Invest in sewer backflow valves to mitigate the risk of sewer system backups.

A provision that many homeowners disregard is the possibility of flying debris. Protect your windows, doors, and skylights, as these can be weak points in your home. Boarding them up using plywood or installing hurricane shutters can be beneficial. Keep in mind that tape does not prevent windows from breaking and, therefore, won't keep wind or rain out of your home.

If you're lucky, you might have ample time to set these in order before a hurricane hits. However, the best practice is to ensure your home remains hurricane-ready all-year-round. Statistically, most hurricane-related home damages can be prevented with the right modifications and quick repairs.

Implementing these modifications can provide you peace of mind that your home is armed against hurricanes. Every bit of reinforcement and every protective measure deployed can mean the difference between weathering the storm and catastrophe.

Ensure that the modifications are up to local floodplain and building codes. When disaster strikes, you can't control it, but you sure can prepare for it. Your home is more than just a building. It's a place full of memories and love. It's worth protecting. And remember, even if the hurricane does cause damage, the key is to stay safe. Houses can be fixed; human lives cannot.

Windows and Shutters

Next on the inspection checklist, let's focus on one of the most vulnerable components of our homes when it comes to hurricanes: the windows. Did you know that high-speed winds aren't the only concern during a hurricane? Flying debris—a real aspect of what we deal with in these storms— can cause serious harm to unprotected windows.

Believe it or not, it's not just about preventing shattered glass from injuring those inside the house, although that's certainly important to avoid. By maintaining the integrity of your windows, you can keep high-pressure winds from entering your home during a storm, which could cause significant structural damage. So let's break down what we need to do.

First off, consider thick, impact-resistant windows. They might cost a sizable penny initially, but in the long run, they could pay off—protecting your home, and even saving you money on your insurance premiums.

Don't assume your current windows are strong enough without doing a check. Ask a professional to evaluate your windows and give you an honest assessment of their ability to withstand a hurricane. If needed, consider arranging for upgraded, storm-ready window installation.

Shutters

Now, let's move on to a more cost-effective approach: shutters. Hurricane shutters are a must-have for any resident living in hurricane-prone areas. They offer an added layer of protection for your windows, eschewing all that extra glass for a cheaper, no less effective, method.

Like everything else in this world, you have choices here too. There are a variety of different types of shutters available, from accordion and Colonial shutters to Bahama and roll-down shutters. Your choice depends on your needs, budget, and the aesthetics of your home. Once installed, ensure you're familiar with how to deploy them when a storm starts churning off the coast.

A more budget-friendly, though labour-intensive, alternative to shutters is cutting plywood boards to cover your windows. Plywood is not as robust as shutters, but it can offer some protection from flying debris. Mark and store the boards so they're easy to find and install when a storm warning is issued.

One key tip: don't wait for the hurricane warning before scrambling to fit your shutters or cut your plywood. Instead, have these storm defenders ready to go at the beginning of hurricane season; that way, when the news tells you about that big, bad storm coming our way, you only have to worry about securing them in place.

Remember, preparation is crucial. Not only will it save you from potential harm, but it will also give you peace of mind as the storm rolls in. Hearing the wind howl and the rain pound is scary enough without worrying about an unsecured window or shutter.

So, are your windows and shutters ready for whatever Mother Nature throws our way? They need to be. It's not just about protecting your property—it's about protecting your family, your neighbors, and your community. Because standing strong in the face of adversity—that's what we do in the West Coast of Florida.

Roof and Structural Integrity

Do you know the phrase "got a sturdy roof over my head?" It's rightly said. Getting through a hurricane means ensuring that the roof above your head is sturdy indeed, not to mention the rest of your house. And that's where we delve into the world of roof and structural integrity. It might seem dull, but it's one of the most critical factors in hurricane preparedness.

When it comes to your home's roof, it's not just about keeping rain out. A secure roof can help prevent wind from entering the house and causing what is known as an "uplift" – a nasty situation where wind causes your roof to fly off. Not cool! - Florida building codes have emphasized this after Hurricane Andrew proved what a hurricane can do to homes. Depending on your home's age, you may need to hire a professional to inspect your roof, looking for loose shingles, unsecured sections, or weak structures that might be a problem in a storm.

Building codes on the West coast of Florida now require hurricane ties, also known as hurricane straps. These small pieces of metal do a hefty job: they help keep your roof attached to the walls of your house during those high gusty winds. Check your attic if you are unsure whether your house has these. If you're unfamiliar with what they look like, or unsure if yours are up to code, it might be a good idea to get a home inspector to check things over.

Beyond your roof, take a long, hard look at your home's structural integrity. It's important to be brutally honest with oneself. If needed, call in an inspector or contractor to take a look. Parts to be particularly wary of include any rotten wood on window frames or doors and cracks in the foundational walls. Unfortunately, these can greatly amplify the chances of damage during a storm.

Additionally, consider what flying debris could do to your home. Trees with dead limbs, old kid's toys in the backyard, outdoor furniture - I'm sure you've got the idea. Remove or securely anchor down anything that could become a projectile in the wind. It's not just about preventing these from damaging your house, but your neighbor's too.

Garage doors, they may seem innocuous, but they're actually among the most vulnerable part of your home in a hurricane. They take a beating from both wind and debris. Make sure they are reinforced to withstand hurricane-force winds. Many aftermarket reinforcement kits are available, and installing one now could save your home later.

So, we've checked the structural integrity of the house, right? Everything seemed alright? Well, not so fast. Don't forget about secondary structures, such as sheds, fences, or pergolas. Wind doesn't discriminate and can damage these structures just as much as your main house. Assess these structures for any needed repairs or reinforcements.

If you're on the coast, you have an added concern — storm surge. Storm surge can wash away even the most well-constructed homes or cause severe flood damage. If you're in a surge zone, elevate critical structures, like electrical panels, as much as possible to avoid water damage.

Roof and structural integrity may not be the most thrilling part of hurricane preparation, but taking the time to ensure your home is as sturdy as possible can make a world of difference when the storm hits. It's about more than property damage - it's about protecting you and your family. So get out there, make those checks, and get ready to weather the storm. Don't forget, as they say, "an ounce of prevention is worth a pound of cure."

Stocking Emergency Supplies

The heart of hurricane preparedness lies in assembling an effective cache of emergency supplies. This stash will function as your lifeboat when the storm hits, and for potentially several days – or even weeks – afterwards. Yes, that's right - supplies to last for weeks. Hurricanes can cause tremendous damage and disruptions, sometimes causing residents to fend for themselves for a considerable duration.

So, where should you start when it comes to stocking up? First off, don't panic-buy. It's essential to shop smart and ahead of time. In the frenzy leading up to a hurricane, store shelves can quickly become bare as people start panic-buying. Start building your supplies ahead of time, piece by piece, so when hurricane warnings pounce, you're already sat comfortably with your hurricane stash, minus the last-minute panic buying stress.

Now let's consider what items should make your must-have list.

Provisions

Food and water top the list of essentials. It's recommended to have a supply of non-perishable food and water to last each person in your household for at least three days but aim for a two-week supply where possible. Remember, canned goods are excellent, but don't forget to stock a manual can opener too!

Health Supplies

Let's keep you healthy during the storm. Include any prescription medicines required by family members, along with a basic first aid kit. This isn't the time for complicated surgical procedures - just enough to deal with minor injuries and basic health needs. Remember to include band-aids, antiseptic wipes, tweezers, medical tape, gauze pads, and any over-the-counter medication you may need.

Power

No one likes being left in the dark, especially during a hurricane. You'd be surprised how much a little light can boost morale when the power is out. Stock up on flashlights, extra batteries, and candles. If you're using candles, remember to exercise caution and never leave them unattended.

Cleaning Supplies

Hand sanitizers, wipes, garbage bags, and similar items are crucial to maintaining hygiene during a prolonged power outage - you'll be thankful you had them met needed. Add these to your emergency supplies list.

Clothing and Bedding

Make sure you have a change of clothing and bedding for each family member. While it's not likely that your clothes or bedding will be destroyed in a hurricane, having a spare clean and dry set can be a true comfort during stressful times. Plus, in the unlikely event that you have to evacuate suddenly, they will be an excellent addition to your emergency evacuation kit.

Other Supplies

Consider other miscellaneous items as well, such as waterproof bags (for important documents), baby supplies (if needed), a multi-tool, duct tape, matches, a whistle (to signal for help), and entertainment items (like books or board games) to keep your spirits up during the storm.

Putting in the effort to stock emergency supplies can make a tremendous difference in how you fare during a hurricane. By preparing ahead of time and maintaining your supplies year-round, you'll not only be ready for a hurricane, you're setting yourself up to thrive during any disaster. You got this, Hurricane Warrior!

Food and Water

Now, let's talk about something that's more on everyone's plate, literally: food and water. Ensuring your family has enough to eat and drink before, during, and after a hurricane is essential. Because the power could go out and regular water sources contaminated, some preparation is indeed in order here.

Big on everyone's mind is: how much food should I stockpile in the event of a hurricane? The good ole rule of thumb tends to ring true: have at least a three-day supply for each family member. Yet, if we're honest with ourselves, a week's worth is safer. Especially if we remember that aftermath phase when everything's trying to recalibrate.

And as for packing the old pantry, remember, you're looking for non-perishable sustenance. Think canned goods like soups, fruits, veggies, and that ever-versatile canned tuna. Also, don't forget the can opener. Dry goods like nuts, trail mix, granola bars, and breakfast cereals make excellent choices too. Simpler might be better in these circumstances.

Easy-to-prep foods like crackers and peanut butter, or rice and dried beans can fill you up in a jiffy, no cooktop required.

Yet as human beings, we can't predict every craving or dietary need. So consider anybody with special dietary requests or restrictions. Someone in your family a diabetic? Got a house full of vegetarian teens? Make sure your preparedness pantry caters to everyone. Not easy, but necessary.

Also, don't forget about comfort foods in stressful situations like these. Familiar foods can offer a sense of normalcy and relieve stress. So slip in a few treats, like cookies, popcorn, or candy. It's not all Spoonful-of-Sugar-Makes-the-Medicine-Go-Down pop psychology, but it can certainly help take the edge off.

Babies and infants have unique nutritional needs. Got a small one in the house? Remember to stock up on pre-mixed baby formula, baby food, and extra bottles.

Don't let's forget our furry friends either. Pet food can be easily overlooked when stocking up. Stockpile at least a week's worth of food and water for Fluffy and Fido too.

Once we have the food situation in hand, let's pivot our attention to that other vital necessity: water. Good old H2O is valuable both for drinking and sanitation purposes. The American Red Cross suggests having a three-day supply of water — that's one gallon per person per day. But when you consider sanitation uses, having more certainly won't hurt.

Don't assume bottled water is the only option. Other containers can store water just as effectively. Anything from collapsible water containers to large, food-grade plastic barrels can do the job. But remember, whichever storage method you opt for, it's essential to treat stored water to protect against bacteria and other contaminants.

You can treat your stored water using a few methods. Boiling is the oldest and somewhat tried-and-true method. But chemicals like iodine or chlorine dioxide tablets can do the trick as well. Just follow the instructions closely.

You'll also need some water for sanitation purposes. This water doesn't need to be as pure as your drinking water, but having a separate supply on hand is crucial. This could be used for everything from washing hands and face to cleaning food prep areas.

All these details might seem a bit overwhelming. But hey, just remember the basics. Stock up on non-perishable foods, allow for special diets, ensure there's enough for everyone (pets included), and treat and store water effectively. Do this, and you'll be well on your way to weathering any hurricane with a good meal in your belly and a refreshing gulp of drink to wash it down.

Coping with the impacts of a hurricane is never an easy task. Yet with some forward-thinking meal planning, and a clear water strategy, you're giving your family the best possible chance to safely and healthily weather the storm.

First Aid Kit

As we delve into the realm of emergency supplies, let's take a moment to turn a keen eye to a pivotal item in any hurricane preparedness kit, the first aid kit. Often underestimated, a robust first aid kit is as essential to your safety during a hurricane as sturdy walls are to your home.

A good starting point for your first aid kit would be sterile dressings and bandages of various sizes to staunch bleeding and dress wounds. You'll also need adhesive tape for securing the dressings. Antiseptic wipes and hydrogen peroxide can be used to cleanse wounds, while antibiotic ointments help to prevent infections. Tweezers can be handy for removing debris from wounds and scissors are useful for cutting tape and clothing. Add in a digital thermometer to monitor body temperature, and a couple of instant cold packs for reducing swelling or pain.

You should also always include a stock of over-the-counter medications. This would include things like pain relievers, anti-diarrhea medication, antacids, and laxatives. Spare eyeglasses and contact lens solution may be helpful for those with vision problems. And remember to put in a couple of doses of any prescription medications that you or your family members can't do without.

There's no telling when a hurricane might hit and how severe it might be. So it pays to think ahead and prepare for more serious medical problems too. This could mean including an emergency blanket to combat hypothermia, a blood pressure kit and even a tourniquet. It's always better to have these items and not need them, than need them and not have them, right? Also, don't forget to pack a first aid instruction booklet, because even the best prepared among us can blank out when facing an alarming situation.

Preparing a first aid kit can feel a bit like a balancing act, where you're trying not to miss out any essentials yet also aiming not to overload the kit. Take a moment to tailor your first aid kit to the unique needs of your family. Do you have infants or elderly individuals in your household? Their needs should be considered as well. Sunscreen, insect repellent, baby supplies, or special senior care items can be packed in a separate bag if your first aid kit doesn't have enough room. At the end of the day, your first aid kit should be as versatile, comprehensive, and personal as your hurricane preparedness plan.

Power and Light Sources

Let's switch gears and talk about your power and light sources during a hurricane. Repeat after me: you can never have too many. When a storm hits, you're likely to lose power at some point, and there's always the possibility that it may take several days for it to be restored. With this in mind, it's essential to plan accordingly to ensure you're never literally left in the dark.

First off, take advantage of the many portable options available for lighting. Things like battery-operated lanterns, flashlights, headlamps, and even glow sticks can be handy for navigating a dark house. Remember, safety is paramount, so no candles or kerosene lamps, please. These pose a fire risk, and that's the last thing you need during a hurricane.

Next up, let's look at power sources. One option to consider, specifically for your major appliances, is a portable generator or a standby generator if your budget allows it. They can power everything from your fridge to your AC, keeping you cool and your food fresh. But remember, generators can be dangerous if misused. Always ensure they are used outdoors, well away from windows and doors, to prevent carbon monoxide poisoning.

A battery backup, or uninterruptible power supply (UPS), can be crucial for your electronics. It provides short-term power during an outage, allowing you to take necessary actions like saving files on your computer or keeping your internet modem and router running for a while.

Investing in portable power banks for your mobile devices can be a lifesaver as well. They are affordable, widely available, and would keep your phones and tablets charged, allowing you to stay connected and informed.

Speaking of staying informed, a battery-powered or hand-crank radio is a must for your hurricane prep kit. It'll be your go-to for updates when power and internet service are down. They also frequently come with a built-in flashlight, and some even have a USB port to charge your mobile devices.

You should also stock up on plenty of batteries for flashlights, radios, and other battery-operated devices, too. And get a variety of sizes because you never know what you might need.

While we're on the subject of batteries, consider investing in rechargeable ones, along with a solar or crank charger. They're economical and eco-friendly and will keep you powered up during prolonged outages.

Finally, we can't forget about cooking. If you've got a gas-powered stove, you'll be good to go. Alternatively, consider a camp stove or a grill, but always follow the manufacturer's guidelines and never use them indoors.

With these power and light sources sorted, you're well on your way to maintaining a safe, well-lit, and fully functional home during a hurricane. Remember, preparation is half the battle, and every little bit counts when Mother Nature decides to flex her muscles.

Chapter 3: Evacuation Strategies

The moment authorities announce an impending hurricane, having a robust evacuation plan should be your top priority. Remember, getting out of harm's way isn't the same as running off in a haste – it's about being systematic and prepared. Your evacuation plan needs to include details like when to leave, where to go, and which route to take. Consider factors such as road closures and the speed of the advancing hurricane. This isn't a trip to the beach, you need to assemble an evacuation kit containing essentials like non-perishable food, water, medicines, and essential documents. Key to this plan is a consideration for every member of your family, including your pets. Believe me, you can't afford to leave Fluffy running around in the gusty winds and flooding waters. Having an all-inclusive evacuation strategy ensures you'll be ready to hit the road in a jiffy, but with everything you'll need, and everyone you love in tow.

Developing an Evacuation Plan

Living on the west coast of Florida, we're no strangers to the possibility of having to evacuate due to a hurricane. But knowing when and how to leave can make all the difference between a smooth retreat and a chaotic exodus. Crafting an effective evacuation plan is akin to armoring yourself for a hurricane. Let's walk through the steps of putting together a solid plan.

Your first task is determining if your home is in an evacuation zone. You might assume you're safe if you're not on the immediate coast, but floods from hurricanes can reach areas well inland. Check with your local government office or websites to find out if you're in a designated evacuation area.

Next up, we're going to identify safe places to go. This could be a public shelter, a hotel, or the homes of family or friends living outside the hurricane risk area. Keep in mind that public shelters should be a last resort due to limited space and resources. Shelters cannot guarantee comfiest set-ups either, and often don't allow pets, so have other options on your list as well.

If you're going to a hotel or motel, make sure it's pet-friendly if you have any animal companions and check their policies on reservations during emergencies. Some establishments may not honor regular reservations during declared emergencies or disaster zones.

- **Plan Multiple Routes:** Next, plot multiple routes to your chosen destination. Why not just one? Because storms aren't considerate of our plans. They can close roads, flood routes or cause other obstacles that may require you to adjust your course. Use physical maps or GPS to help you plot the easiest and quickest routes.

You also need to establish a communication plan. Choose a family member or friend who lives out of the hurricane impact zone to be your contact person, and make sure everyone in your household knows their phone number. This person can keep track of your whereabouts and be the touchpoint for everyone in your family to minimize confusion. Remember, cell service can be spotty during storms, so don't rely entirely on your phone.

Now, after plotting your destination and routes, it's time to focus on what you need to take with you. Create a checklist with essential items like vital documents, emergency supplies, pet necessities, and some comforts like clothing and toiletries. This list will ensure you don't forget anything in the chaotic rush of an evacuation.

- **Practice Makes Perfect:** Don't wait until the hurricane arrives to put your plan into action. Try a dry run of your evacuation plan, including packing your essentials, driving your identified routes, and ensuring that everyone knows the plan. Practice may feel silly— until you're facing an actual evacuation, at which point you'll be relieved you took the time.

Preparing for the financial implications of evacuation is another crucial step. Consider setting aside some cash in your emergency kit. ATMs might not work due to power outages, and not all places may accept credit or debit cards during a crisis. It's also wise to check whether your insurance covers evacuation and accommodation expenses.

The final step, and a crucial one, is to stay informed. Regular updates from local authorities will tell you when an evacuation order is issued, and what specific steps you should take. Either via radio, TV, apps or social media, be sure to have a couple of ways to receive these updates.

You may wonder: when should you actually evacuate? In short — when local authorities tell you to. They have the best understanding of the threat the storm presents. But if you notice that roads are already getting busy or that a storm is approaching faster than predicted, you might want to leave ahead of an official evacuation order.

One point we must stress, however, is this: once an evacuation order is issued, don't delay. Ignoring evacuation orders poses a serious threat to your life and the lives of your family. Also, bear in mind that overlooking evacuation orders may stall emergency services that might be needed elsewhere.

Developing a solid evacuation plan is a hefty task, but it's essential to ensure you and your loved ones stay safe and secure during a hurricane. Preparation today can make a world of difference in the face of an oncoming storm.

Being ready and having a plan doesn't mean you live in fear, but rather that you live prepared. As we know here on the Florida West Coast, the sea doesn't rule us, but it does sometimes push us, and we need to be ready to move when it does.

Choosing an Evacuation Route

The topic of your evacuation route needs to be right up there on the list when you're piecing together your game plan for hurricane season. The Florida Division of Emergency Management develops official evacuation routes in response to tropical weather threats. Though these are pretty well thought out, personalizing your individual route is a smart move.

To start with, consider where you'd head if the warning to leave came through. Your destination might be a friend's place, a relative's house, or a motel in a safe zone. Whichever it is, have a practiced route mapped out to that destination with at least one back-up plan in case of potential obstacles, such as flooded roads or intense traffic.

User-friendly tools like Google Maps or the Waze app could be your allies in spotting traffic jams or road closures.

However, remember that in a real evacuation, digital maps might be hectic at best or not functional at worst. So having a good old-fashioned printed map in your evacuation kit is a lifesaver.

Now, once your destination and routes are defined, consider timing. Ideally, you want to be on the road well before the storm hits. Timing matters as just a few hours can make the difference between an easy ride and a gridlock nightmare. Make sure to factor in extra road time to your trip – trust me, it's not something you want to rush.

Let's say that worst-case scenario happens: you're on the road, and the conditions take a turn for the worse. You hit traffic, or a route is blocked, and the storm is almost on top of you. That's where your backup routes come into use. Diversifying your plans using knowledge of the local area can save your life in this kind of situation.

Sometimes official evacuation routes can get pretty congested, so knowing a few less-traveled roads could be of real benefit. You're shooting for a balance here, though; don't risk taking difficult or dangerous routes because they're less busy. Safety first, always.

For your route planning, make a point of identifying service stations, food stops, and rest areas. Having places to refuel, grab some food, or rest may seem minor now, but when it's in the middle of an evacuation, they could be godsend locations. Make sure to check the availability of these stops, especially in the event of a large-scale evacuation.

Also, don't forget the importance of communication. Have an agreed-upon method in place to stay in contact with loved ones or neighbors. This way, you can share information about travel conditions, help each other out if something unexpected happens, and just generally support each other through a tough situation.

Lastly, remember that the best evacuation route is the one you never have to take. Always follow the recommendations of local authorities relating to evacuations. If they say it's safe to stay, hunker down with your hurricane kit at home. But if they recommend leaving, having that route chosen, practiced, and ready to go will make a world of difference.

Preparing an Evacuation Kit

Ah, the evacuation kit! This little gem of preparedness can't be underestimated. When the hurricane sirens wail and you're hustling to get your family to safety, this compact collection of essentials is going to be your best friend. But, how do you pack the perfect evacuation kit?

Though it might seem overwhelming, it doesn't have to be. Think of it as a well-packed suitcase for a three-day trip, except the destination isn't a fun getaway, but a route to survival. You need to stay focused and cover all bases, packing essentials that would keep you comfortable in case of a hurricane evacuation.

Water and Food. This is the backbone of your evacuation kit. You should have a gallon of water per person per day for at least three days. Non-perishable canned food, dried fruits and nuts, and high-energy bars come in handy. Don't forget to pack a manual can opener. Remember, you're packing for at least three days, although a week's supply would be even better.

Clothing and Outdoor Gear. Pack a change of clothes for each person. Think about comfort, durability, and protection from elements. Don't forget sturdy shoes. Lightweight tents, sleeping bags and blankets can offer quick shelter and warmness, meanwhile hats and sunglasses can give you protection from the sun.

Light and Tools. Portable lanterns and flashlights with extra batteries help you navigate in the dark. A multi-tool Swiss knife, ropes, duct tape and plastic tarps can come handy for various situations.

First Aid Kit. A basic first aid kit with band aids, antiseptic wipes, tweezers, medical tape, pain relievers, and other essentials can handle minor mishaps. Don't forget prescription medications and copies of prescriptions, if required.

Hygiene Items. Personal hygiene is critical in maintaining health, so pack travel-size toiletries including toothpaste, hand sanitizer, feminine supplies, toilet paper, and moist towelettes.

Documents and Cash. Important documents – like driver's licenses, social security cards, health insurance info, and copies of key legal documents – should be kept in a waterproof, portable container. Also, keep a reasonable amount of cash and change on hand. ATMs might not be working.

Entertainment. This might seem unnecessary, but trust me, it's not. A deck of cards, travel board games, or books can provide much-needed distraction, especially for young ones.

Once you've gathered everything, it's best to pack the kit in a set of easy-to-carry containers like a duffel bag or a couple of backpacks. Distribute the weight evenly among your family members based on their capacity.

Remember, prepare your kit early—like before the hurricane season starts. Not much of a kit if you're scrambling to assemble it as the storm barrels down, right?

However, don't just prepare it and forget it. Check your evacuation kit at least once a year, preferably at the start of the hurricane season. Replace expired food and medications, and update documents or cash as necessary.

Lastly, your kit needs to evolve as your family does. If you bring in a new additions, furry or otherwise, you'll need to add to your kit to accommodate them. The same goes for when the kids grow older – switch out toys, increase food and water supply, swap out clothes for larger ones, and so forth.

Now, with each successive step of packing the items listed above, you're building an insurance of sorts—an assurance that no matter which way the wind blows, you've got a plan and the means to implement it.

As we dart towards the next chapter, keep the essence of this prep mantra swirling in your mainframe: Plan, pack, evolve, and most importantly, stay safe.

Pet Evacuation: Don't Forget Fluffy!

We've been talking a lot about human survival during a hurricane, but let's not forget about the furry or feathered members of the family. Your pets depend on you for their safety during a storm, and there are several steps you can take to ensure they're safe and sound.

One thing's for sure: you can't simply let Fluffy or Fido wander on their own. Pets often panic in extreme weather situations and might run away or hide. Not to mention, the harsh weather could be harmful or even fatal to them. Your evacuation plan must include your pets. Some evacuation shelters won't allow pets for health and safety reasons, so it's vital to research and identify pet-friendly shelters in your area ahead of time. And remember, most shelters require you to keep pets in carriers or crates, so make sure you have these items ready.

Prepping a pet evacuation kit in conjunction with your own is also key. Your pet's kit should include food, water, any necessary medications, a leash, a favorite toy to comfort them, and importantly, copies of their vet records and vaccination history. It's not uncommon for shelters or hotels to need proof that your pet is up-to-date on shots.

It's also a good idea to have your pet microchipped if they aren't already. In the chaos of evacuation or a storm, pets can easily get lost. A microchip increases the chances of your pet being returned to you if they get lost. It's a small investment that could make a big difference in an emergency.

Remember, in the midst of a hurricane, what's safest for you is safest for your pets. They're part of the family, after all. Keep them with you, and make sure your emergency plans account for their specific needs. The better prepared you are, the more likely it is that everyone, including Fluffy, will make it through the storm unscathed.

Chapter 4: Riding Out the Storm

Now, imagine the uncertainty of when the sky turns vengeful, and it feels like you've become the bullseye of a temperamental weather pattern. We've talked about tying down, boarding up, and prepping to vamoose. But suppose the situation isn't bad enough to warrant an evacuation, or perhaps circumstances didn't permit it. It's venue change time, folks. Your hurricane party just turned into a "how to survive the blowout" soiree. It becomes a strategic game on our home turf, and staying safe becomes the number one priority. As the wind begins to howl like a pack of famished wolves, understanding when it's safer to stay rather than hit the road is critical. Sure, your house isn't a medieval castle, but with appropriate pre-storm planning, it won't crumble like a house of cards either. We'll delve into the concept of safe rooms and shelters, the cozy last-resort bunkers designed to withstand winds that'll toss your backyard flamingos like frisbees. Here, we ponder the control of utilities like gas, water, and electricity during the storm. Flicking that wrong switch could be like turning a horror flick into a reality tv show. And just as crucial, we'll equip you with guidelines on staying updated with hurricane alerts and updates throughout the storm. No, it won't just be about gluing your eyes to the TV or stressing your radio's volume button, there are more tech savvy ways, trust me. The tale begins with staying hunkered down at home and ends with bracing a storm on this very turf. Your home is your castle and this chapter is the blueprint of your fortress.

When to Stay and When to Go

One of the most pressing questions you'll face when a hurricane is on the horizon is whether to stay put or evacuate. This decision is a critical one, as it can significantly impact your safety.

In some situations, staying at home is the best option. This might be the case if you're far enough inland that you're not at immediate risk of storm surge or flooding, and your home is well-built and able to withstand high winds. You should have enough supplies to last for at least a week, including food, water, medications, and emergency items such as a first-aid kit, flashlights, and batteries.

However, other circumstances might call for immediate evacuation. If you're in a flood-prone or low-lying area, staying at home could put you at serious risk. Additionally, anyone living in a mobile home should plan to evacuate, regardless of the storm's strength or projected path. Mobile homes are not designed to withstand hurricane force winds.

It's also a good idea to consider your personal situation. If you have a medical condition that requires regular care or could become serious without electricity, you might want to plan on evacuating, even if you're not in a mandatory evacuation zone. The same goes for those with young children, elderly family members, or pets.

When you make the choice to evacuate, timing is critical. Ideally, you should leave well ahead of the storm's arrival. Highways can become crowded and slow-moving as more people decide to evacuate, and you don't want to be caught on the road in the middle of a hurricane. Pay close attention to updates from local officials and weather forecasts, and leave as soon as an evacuation order is issued.

If you do decide to stay at home, take steps to ensure you're as protected as possible. Be sure all windows and doors are securely closed and shuttered, bring any outdoor furniture or other objects inside, and make sure you know where all your emergency supplies are. It's also a good idea to choose a safe room in your house where you and your family can huddle during the worst of the storm.

If you're not in a mandatory evacuation zone but still decide to leave, don't forget that you'll need a place to go. This could be a hotel or motel in a safer area, a shelter set up by local officials, or the home of a friend or family member outside the hurricane's path.

When evacuating, remember to take only what you need and what you can't replace. This includes important documents, medications, supplies for your pets, and a few changes of clothing. Leave the rest behind—you can replace most items, but you can't replace a life lost because you spent too much time packing.

Determining whether to stay or go can be a difficult decision, but preparation and information are your best friends. By having a plan in place, understanding the risks associated with your specific area, and carefully monitoring the storm, you'll be well-equipped to make the best decision for you and your family.

And remember, officials don't issue evacuation orders lightly. If you're told to evacuate, there's a good reason for it. Follow their instructions swiftly and calmly, and do your part to keep yourself and your community safe.

In conclusion, be prepared, stay informed, and remain vigilant. When a hurricane is looming, understanding when to stay and when to go can quite literally be a matter of life and death.

Safe Rooms and Shelters

If you've decided to ride out the storm at home, you'll want to identify a safe room where you can retreat to if the hurricane intensifies. Generally, these are interior rooms without windows like hallways, bathrooms, closets, or even basements if your house has one. It's highly suggested to pick a room that's situated on the first floor and one that offers easy access to essentials like the bathroom and the kitchen.

Create an internal shelter by reinforcing a small, windowless, interior room. Use sturdy furniture against the doors, put mattresses against the walls, and cover yourself with a mattress or sleeping bag. You're looking for as many layers between you and the blowing, swirling, projectile-laden tornado winds as you can reasonably create.

Bear in mind that safe rooms are not a go-to for all hurricanes, particularly the high category ones. These ruthless storms can cause more damage and it's always safer to evacuate when your local authorities' mandate it. Especially if you're living on the coast, in a mobile home, or in flood-risk territory.

While preparing a safe room, stock it with a survival kit that includes the essentials - food, water, medical supplies, important documents, cash, clothing, and bedding. Also, remember to have a battery-powered or hand-crank radio to stay informed about storm updates. If circumstances get worse, it might be needed to stay in the safe room for a prolonged period.

Another vital resource during a hurricane is a community shelter. When officials recommend evacuating, or if the house doesn't have robust structural integrity, heading to a shelter is a viable option. Some residents may even need to evacuate to shelters if their homes are in evacuation zones or flood-prone areas. Shelters are usually set up in places like schools, churches, or community centers.

Remember, living in a hurricane shelter can be testing. Space is limited and conditions might not be the most comfortable. But it's a whole lot safer than bearing the brunt of a hurricane. Be ready to bring along your own blankets, pillows, and sleepwear. Keep a store of essential needs like personal care items, medicines, hand sanitizer, and masks.

Wherever you opt to hole up, whether it's a safe room in your home or a community shelter, ensure that you're stocked with enough supplies for at least a week. This gives you ample coverage for the duration of the storm, and some extra if access to resources is temporarily blocked.

Usually, local authorities will provide information about shelter locations and their capacity. To keep yourself updated, monitor local news or relevant apps. You could also compile a list of potential community shelters ahead of time in case of last-minute panics.

Don't forget, pets are an important part of your family too. Not all community shelters accept pets, so it's crucial to plan ahead. There are pet-friendly shelters available, or you can make arrangements with a local veterinary office, pet boarding facility, or animal rescue organization that can take care of your furry friends until you're safe to return home.

Overall, your safety and the safety of your loved ones is paramount. It's okay if your safe room isn't perfect or your community shelter is a bit crowded, as long as you're out of harm's way. Use these tips to prepare a safe room or find a hurricane shelter. Stay vigilant, act quickly, and you'll be in control, despite the chaos.

Utility Safety: Gas, Water, and Electricity

Alright, so you've made it through prepping your home, stocking up on supplies and you've got your evacuation plan in place. Now, let's talk a little about utility safety before, during, and after a hurricane. We're specifically going to dive into gas, water, and electricity, as these are the ones most likely to be affected during such intense natural events.

First up, we have gas. Outages and leaks can happen, so it's crucial to understand how to safely manage your home's gas supply. If you smell a rotten egg odor or hear a hissing sound, that could be a natural gas leak, which is dangerous if not addressed. To be safe, don't light any open flames and avoid any switches or appliances that could cause a spark. If you can, turn off the gas at the main shut-off valve, usually found outside near the gas meter. But get this, never try to fix a gas leak yourself. Call your gas company or 911 after you've left the house.

Water safety is also a vital aspect to cover. You see, hurricanes can disrupt water systems, and contaminate drinking sources. Listen to local authorities for boil water notices or use bottled water until you're certain that local water is safe. Limit toilet flushing or other discretionary water use during outages to keep as much uncontaminated water stored as possible.

Let's shift gears to electricity, an integral part of our daily lives and a crucial resource during emergencies. Hurricanes often knock out power lines, causing outages that can last from a few hours to a few weeks. To stay safe, keep away from downed power lines and report them immediately.

Plus, always have flashlights and batteries on hand to avoid using candles, which could cause a fire.

On the subject of power, your home's electrical system can also be a concern. If you're expecting a flood, disconnect appliances to prevent potential electrical shock when power is restored. And here's a big one: never step in standing water where you know there's an active electrical source nearby.

Speaking of floods, generators can be life-savers in extended outages, but they can also pose risks. Never run a generator indoors due to the risk of carbon monoxide poisoning. Also, remember to always run generators at a safe distance outside and away from windows, doors, and vent openings.

Surges can happen when the power comes back on, potentially damaging plugged-in electronics. You can prevent this by unplugging unnecessary appliances and charging phones or laptops in short bursts instead of waiting until they're fully charged.

Post-storm, don't be in a rush to turn everything back on. Listen to local reports to know when it's safe to restart utilities. Also, you'll want to inspect utility lines and systems for damage before use, especially gas lines. When in doubt, reach out to a professional for inspection and repair.

In conclusion, utilities are precious commodities that become even more vital during extreme weather. Learning the proper safety procedures can save lives and make hurricane experiences less traumatic. We can't control the storm, but we can command our responses to it, and that's the key. Carry this knowledge with you, and you'll be that much more prepared to tackle the hurricane season like a champ.

Up next, we'll talk about how to stay informed and connected to the world when it feels like you're fighting a hurricane solo.

How to Keep Informed

Taking a storm by stride involves more than merely amassing a stash of food, water, and emergency supplies. It's also essential to make a concerted effort to stay informed about the hurricane's progression during the build-up, whilst it's in full force, and as the aftermath unfolds. Knowledge paired with preparation is your strongest defense, so let's dive into the best ways to keep informed.

Start your information-finding mission by tuning into local radio and television stations. Look out for broadcasts from reliable sources such as the National Weather Service (NWS), or your local news outlets. This age-old method still proves to be one of the most effective in getting real-time info about oncoming storms. But be sure to have a battery-powered or hand-cranked radio at hand, in case you lose power.

Additionally, the NWS also operates NOAA Weather Radio All Hazards (NWR), a nationwide network broadcasting live weather information. NWR works around the clock, providing comprehensive weather-related updates, including detailed emergency information such as hurricane warnings or evacuation details.

The Internet and social media platforms are also valuable tools in this tech-savvy era. They provide a constant flow of updates from organizations like the National Hurricane Center, which posts storm-tracking data, satellite images, and weather forecasts online. Twitter, Facebook, and even

Instagram are used by many local communities and emergency management departments to disseminate information quickly.

Don't forget the wealth of hurricane-specific apps available for smartphone users, too. Free apps like the Hurricane Tracker and the American Red Cross Hurricane App can provide blow-by-blow alerts. These savvy resources also offer preparedness tips, evacuation routes, open shelter locations, and recovery information.

Maintaining open lines of communication with your neighbors is another key component to staying informed. Community can prove invaluable during crisis situations, sharing the burden and acting as a collective unit. On top of that, surrounding yourself with familiar faces can offer an immense degree comfort in times of uncertainty. A hurricane watch party, anyone?

Besides local coverage, pay attention to national media outlets as well. Unlike local news, national sources are less likely to face disruption from the storm and can continue to provide essential updates.

Let's not forget our trusty phone. Automation has made it easy to receive text-based weather updates and warnings from local and state emergency management officials. Check online how to sign up for these services — they could be a real lifeline.

Keep in mind that information can change quickly, especially during a severe weather event. Double check any information you receive, especially if it sounds alarming or implausible. The confusion dodgy information may sow is the last thing you need during a storm.

The bottom line? Stay alert, stay updated, and stay safe. Every hurricane is unique, and the more we know, the better we can respond. Understanding the storm's movement, size, and potential impact will allow you to make informed decisions about evacuation, sheltering in place, and ensuring the safety of your loved ones. The power is in your hands — or in this case, your radio, TV, and smartphone!

Chapter 5: Communications

The impending storm isn't just brewing in the atmosphere, it's also spinning up a whirlwind of buzz on your phone, TV, and radio. Not all of it will be useful, though. Understanding how to sort through the input, and even contribute your own, is key. Establishing a communication plan can keep you connected with loved ones and up-to-date with crucial updates and alerts. Start by compiling a list of emergency numbers and contacts, including local law enforcement, emergency services, weather stations, hospitals, and nearby shelters. And yes, there's an app for that. Actually, there are many that could save your life, from weather forecasters and hurricane trackers to first aid guides and survival tips. Some even allow your loved ones to track your location during a disaster (an obvious help if you get lost). Keep in mind, though, like a fussy toddler, the internet can be temperamental during a storm. Cue radio, satellite phones, and — the timeless classic — landlines. By incorporating an array of comm tools into your hurricane plan, you can ensure that you're wired for whatever the storm decides to throw at you.

Setting Up a Communication Plan

In the middle of a hurricane, impeccable communication can be the difference between confusion and clarity, between danger and safety. Therefore, it's essential to have a detailed and reliable communication plan in place.

First off, it's crucial to decide on a primary mode of communication. Each family member should keep a list of emergency phone numbers including but not limited to, local emergency services, neighbors, and family friends. Consider designating an out-of-state contact as group contact, as local communication lines may be overwhelmed or unavailable during the storm.

Next, let's focus on communication modes. While we're used to relying heavily on our cell phones, it's vital to consider alternate methods of communication during a hurricane. A battery-operated or crank-powered weather radio can provide critical, timely information when the power's out and your phone's battery is dead. Consider investing in one for your family's safety.

You might also want to consider two-way radios. In scenarios where cell service is spotty or non-existent, these can provide a reliable way to keep in touch with family members or close neighbors. Remember, plan for the worst but hope for the best.

If you're separated from family during the hurricane, it can create a significant amount of stress. It's essential to designate a pre-determined meeting place in case your home isn't safe or accessible. This could be a local community center, a relative's house, or some other agreed-upon location.

Here's something not everyone thinks about - communication for those who may not speak English or have a hearing impairment. Make sure any communication plan you set up can accommodate their needs, as well. This can include learning some basic sign language or carrying a phrasebook for those who speak different languages.

It's important to discuss and rehearse this communication plan with your family, and review it every hurricane season. Familiarity can significantly reduce stress levels during a hurricane and ensure that everyone knows what to do and how to remain in contact. Make sure all family members have a copy of this plan and keep one in an easily accessible emergency kit, too.

And what about when you can't make a call or send a text? It might be old school, but a written note can let others know where you've gone if you've had to evacuate your home. Leave a note behind---secure and protected from the elements---detailing where you're heading and who is with you.

Looking into digital solutions, various apps and tools can help maintain communication in the midst of a storm. We'll delve into these more in the Chapter on Useful Apps and Websites.

Also, while social media often gets bad press, it can be a lifesaver in a hurricane situation. It can provide real-time updates on the storm's progress, and let friends and family know you're safe. Many services such as Facebook have safety check-in features that you can use to quickly reassure your network.

Emails, too, can serve as a useful tool. A quick email can inform a whole group of people about your safety and plans. Plus, emails can often be pushed through slower internet connections—connections not quick enough for phone calls or video chats.

Keep in mind, the best plans are adaptable. While it may not be possible to plan for every scenario, having a flexible communication plan that considers different possibilities can significantly improve your resilience to hurricanes.

Lastly, remember that information is a two-way street. As you're feeding information to your friends and family about your situation, be sure to also listen to what they have to say.

They may have valuable information or advice about the current state of affairs.

In short, setting up a communication plan isn't just about talking, it's about listening, planning, and adapting. And that, in turn, could be the key to keeping everyone safe and sound.

Useful Apps and Websites

Living on the West Coast of Florida, you're all too aware of the power of Mother Nature. When hurricane season rolls around, it's essential to have every tool at your disposal to keep you and your loved ones safe. In the modern age, we're blessed with a variety of apps and websites to aid in this quest. Here's a rundown of some crucial platforms to keep under your belt.

Let's start with apps first. One of your staunchest allies is the 'National Weather Service' (NWS) app. NWS provides up-to-the-minute weather updates, alerts and advisories, which you can personalize to your specific location. Its stellar interface makes it easy to keep tabs on hurricane development and progression.

Next up, the 'Red Cross Emergency' app. Besides offering real-time weather alerts, this app also provides comprehensive details on what to do before, during and after a hurricane. With practical advice, interactive quizzes, and step-by-step guides, you'll be well-prepared for whatever comes your way.

A must-have in any arsenal is 'Zello'. A walkie-talkie app, Zello allows for instant communication with friends, family, and even rescue services. It's proved its worth during previous hurricanes with its fast, efficient updates and alerts. Just remember to keep your devices charged.

Then we've got 'GasBuddy', a nifty little app for anyone preparing to evacuate. It keeps track of gas stations along your route and provides updates on availability, ensuring you stay fueled up and ready to move. Perfect to keep the stress levels down during those crucial moments.

Another brilliant app is 'Nextdoor'. It's like a digital grassroots community forum connecting you with your neighbors. It's great for sharing information, tips, and resources during a crisis.

Moving on to useful websites, 'National Hurricane Center' is top of the list. Run by the US Government, it provides a comprehensive view of all tropical cyclone activity and serves forecasts to help you stay informed about any impending storms.

The 'Florida Division of Emergency Management' website is a gold mine of resources. Here you can find information about storm watches and warnings, evacuation orders, shelter locations, and post-storm recovery assistance.

'Weather.com' needs no introduction. The hurricane section provides valuable updates, storm trackers, and educational articles.

'Ready.gov' is an extremely helpful site with all the prep info you could ever need. They have a specific section for hurricanes explaining how to set up disaster kits, make evacuation plans, and much more.

For those who might need emergency housing, Airbnb's 'Open Homes' platform can be a godsend. This allows people to offer their homes free of charge to those displaced by natural disasters. Worth checking out if you find yourself in a tough spot.

The serious stuff aside, we also recommend queuing up a few light-hearted websites for when the nerves start to fray. Streaming platforms like 'Netflix' or 'Hulu' can provide comforting distraction during those anxious hours of waiting.

Keeping these apps and websites at your fingertips can go a long way towards easing the stress that comes with hurricane season. But remember, technology is just one part of the puzzle. Good preparation, a clear plan, and - above all - sticking together, will see you through anything Mother Nature throws your way.

Make sure to store these apps and bookmark these websites in your device, because when the storm hits, you want all these tools ready to go. Be sure to familiarize yourself with their usage before the hurricane season, so rest assured, when the time comes, you'll know exactly what to do.

Remember, information empowers. In this age of digital connectivity, make it work for you, your family, and your community. Stay safe, Florida.

Emergency Numbers and Contacts

Emergencies can hit without warning, and when they do, having all the relevant contacts and numbers at your fingertips is crucial. Here in the West Coast of Florida, we're no strangers to hurricanes. Keeping an updated list of emergency numbers and contacts is one of your number one priorities to ensure your safety and survival during a hurricane. Not only does this involve authorities such as the police, fire departments, and medical services, but also utility companies, neighbors, and family members.

It's critical to write down a list of emergency contacts, including numbers for the local police and fire departments, local hospitals, and utility services. Also, don't forget about poison control and road and traffic report services. It's also a good idea to include non-emergency numbers, including your insurance company, local TV and radio stations, and your child's school, if applicable.

Local Police and Fire Departments: These are the immediate contacts for any emergency. Ensure you have the direct line to your town's Police Department and Fire Department. Remember, these numbers are not a substitute for 911 in life-threatening situations.

Local Hospitals: In addition to the emergency services number 911, make sure to have a direct line to the hospital closest to you in case you need to reach them about a non-immediate emergency.

Utility Services: Power outages and disrupted water supply are common during a hurricane. Having the direct line to your Gas, Electric, and Water companies, can get you updates and advise on how to handle these situations, especially when there are live power lines down or flooding involved.

Part of your local survival network are your neighbors. In addition to emergency services, ensure you have the contact information of close neighbors. After a storm, community members may be the first to provide help before professional responders arrive.

In the frenzy of a hurricane hitting, one of the very first things that may get upended is our ability to communicate with our loved ones. This is why it's essential to ensure you have written down the contact details of close family members, friends, and anyone else you'd need to communicate with in the event of a hurricane.

Remember, your mobile phone battery won't last indefinitely, especially in prolonged power cuts. Why not take an old-school approach and make a physical copy of relevant numbers? A small, laminated card or waterproof pouch can be a powerful tool in your emergency kit. Also, it's recommended to provide this info to all of your family members, including kids and the elderly.

We can't predict exactly when or where a hurricane will strike. But we can prepare for it. Having a well-thought-out set of emergency contacts in a readily accessible format is critical for the safety and peace of mind of you and your family. Don't forget to update your contacts regularly and ensure that your family members have a copy of these listings too.

In the upcoming sections, we'll take a closer look at how to financially and legally prepare for a hurricane, from understanding your insurance policies to securing essential documents. Later, we'll delve into the community resources available in times of need and discuss special considerations for families with children, senior citizens, disabled individuals, and pets. Stay tuned.

Chapter 6: Financial and Legal Preparedness

While preparing your home and family for hurricanes is vital, don't forget about another key area: your financial and legal preparedness. Think about it like this: a storm could leave your home in shambles, and as much as that'd be hard to handle, it's even harder if you can't quickly access your insurance information or other essential documents to start the recovery process. And let's not even start about the headache of figuring out your bank and credit card details while you're in a temporary shelter. So, first order of business: get to understand your insurance. Know what your policy covers and what it doesn't; hurricane damage, flooding, and other types of post-hurricane sagas each have their own nuances. You also need to protect your essential documents. Invest in a fire and water-resistant lock box for things like deeds, wills, identification, and financial documents. And lastly, create a financial emergency kit - a stash of cash and important information like contact info for your financial advisors, banks, and insurance agent, can be a lifesaver. Preparing for the worst isn't just a physical endeavor, it's a financial and legal one too.

Understanding Your Insurance

Now that we've walked through what a hurricane is and how to prepare for it, let's delve into a topic that may seem complex at first - insurance. This involves figuring out just what your policy covers, what it doesn't, and how to keep everything in order for if or when a hurricane hits.

First thing's first – you've got to understand your policy. This means knowing the definitions, coverages, and exclusions. It seems like a lot, right? But don't stress, we'll break it down:

- **Definitions** – This is where you'll find your insurance lingo explained. For example, what they mean by "actual cash value" vs. "replacement cost."

- **Coverages** – This part outlines what your insurance company will pay for after a disaster. Are you covered for wind damage? Water damage? What about temporary living costs if you have to evacuate?

- **Exclusions** – As you can probably guess, this section lists what won't be covered. This might include certain kinds of water damage.

The second big piece is understanding the difference between replacement cost vs. actual cash value. This determines how much money you'll get if something in your home is damaged or destroyed. Replacement cost is the amount it would take to replace or rebuild your home or repair damages with materials of similar kind and quality. Actual cash value, on the other hand, is the amount it would take to repair or replace damage to your home after depreciation.

Don't let the terms intimidate you. They're just ways of calculating the hit your wallet might take if a hurricane comes to town. Trust me; you'll want to know this stuff ahead of time.

Into the nitty-gritty of your policy, you need to know what kind of perils you're covered for. A peril is simply insurance jargon for a specific risk or cause of loss covered by your policy, such as a fire, windstorm, or theft. Your policy will explicitly state whether it offers *all-risk coverage* (where all perils are covered unless specifically excluded) or *named perils coverage* (only the perils named in the policy are covered).

Now, the tricky part – hurricanes aren't just about wind damage. They bring a lot of water too. But here's the catch: while most homeowners insurance covers wind damage, many policies don't cover flood damage. Yeah, you read that right. If a hurricane sends a tidal wave into your living room, your standard insurance policy might not cover it.

But no need to hit the panic button just yet. There's a thing called flood insurance, and you might need it if you live in the Sunshine State. These policies are generally separate from your usual homeowner's insurance and are often provided through the National Flood Insurance Program (NFIP).

Okay, so you've got a grasp on policy coverage. The next essential step is documenting your belongings. This can help prove the value of what you owned if your possessions are damaged or destroyed. Videos, photos, and an itemized list of major belongings can all be helpful. Store this information in a safe place and consider making a digital copy to have an extra layer of security.

Next up is deductible, another term that gets thrown around in the insurance world. It's the amount of money you agree to pay out of pocket before your insurance coverage kicks in. Higher deductibles often mean lower premiums, but you want to make sure you can afford to pay the deductible should disaster strike.

One more thing—and it's important too—once your policy is in place, review it regularly, especially when you make substantial changes to your home. Remember, anything from installing a new roof to building an addition could change your policy's coverage needs or premiums.

Now that you've got the lay of the land in insurance-ville (hey, just think of it as a less fun version of Disneyland), you can breathe a sigh of relief. You've taken a key step in hurricane preparedness. But remember, insurance is your backstop—it's not your first line of defense. That's why we'll be digging into how to prepare, plan and stay safe in the coming sections.

Okay, that's a wrap on this section. You've just mastered the basics of your insurance. Not so bad, right? Gold star for you!

Important Documents to Protect

We've discussed a lot about physical preparedness, but let's turn our focus on something equally important - paperwork. Not the most thrilling topic, I agree, but crucial in the aftermath of a hurricane. Let's delve into the details of what documents you'll want to have secured and why they're important.

Your identification documents - This includes driver's licenses, national identity cards, passports or even birth certificates. These are used to support and re-establish your identity if required. They can also expedite the process of obtaining relief funds or applying for lost documents.

Proof of residence - Having a document evidencing where you live, such as a utility bill, a signed lease, or a mortgage statement, can be critical when applying for disaster relief or insurance claims. Remember, this needs to have your present address on it.

Medical and health records - Records of known allergies, prescription details, medical conditions, and insurance cards can aid in receiving the proper medical attention in case of emergencies. Vital when regular healthcare providers may not be available after a hurricane, and you're relying on emergency services.

Legal documents - Here, we're talking about wills, power of attorney documents, and living wills. Although these may not be needed immediately, securing them can save you from future headaches. Imagine dealing with probate court amidst a hurricane recovery, not a comforting thought, is it?

Property documents - Having proof of home ownership, or renters' agreements can simplify the insurance claim process post-hurricane. This category also includes car titles, and other property documents so they're accessible when you need them most.

Now, you've got this pile of crucial documents compiled, you may wonder, "What's the best way to protect them?" Well, options range depending on how far you want to go. Both digital and physical safety measures can provide an extra level of security.

For digital storage, scan your critical documents and save them in a secure cloud service, or on a portable hard drive. Ensure this digital format is encrypted and password protected. Include a USB stick with the encrypted files in your evacuation supplies. If cloud services seem too complex, email them to yourself or a trusted person who could print them out if necessary.

For physical safety, invest in a waterproof and fire-resistant safe for your home. This won't safeguard against every event, but will offer a basic level of protection and peace of mind. You might want to consider keeping your original documents in a safety deposit box in a bank if you have one.

Last but not least, make sure all family members or delegates are aware of where these documents are stored. An emergency scenario isn't an ideal time for a treasure hunt!

In conclusion, protecting important documents may not be an adrenaline-pumped task, but it's an aspect of hurricane readiness that we can't ignore. So, let's give it the importance it deserves, secure those vital papers, and we'll be a step further in our preparedness mission.

Creating a Financial Emergency Kit

You've got your home ready, your evac routes planned, and your communication lines open. Perfect preparation! Now, let's step into a slightly different domain - your financials. In the chaos of a cyclone, it's easy to lose track of your financial situation, which can be equally daunting. Having a financial emergency kit ready can make this a bit less stressful.

First things first, what even is a financial emergency kit? It's a secure, ready-to-grab repository of all your important financial documents. This isn't just for hurricanes, mind you. It comes handy during any emergency that might force you to leave your home immediately.

Imagine the hurricane has passed, and you've returned home. Your house was lucky this time, minimal damage! But surprise, your banking institution has been impacted by the storm and cannot operate. Though organizations have their backup strategies, disruptions can still happen. Having personal copies of your account numbers could save you a headache.

So, what should you include in this financial kit? Start with basics like hard copies of your IDs – driving license, social security card, and passport. Make sure you've all the necessary insurance policies – health, home, life, car, and flood (especially flood!). Having a physical copy of these can be an absolute lifesaver.

The next set of documents are related to your assets and debts. Home deeds and mortgage papers, car titles, proof of loans - keep them all in there. Don't forget your rental agreements or lease papers if you're renting. They're your proof that you have a legal right to live there, and they might prove helpful if disputes arise after a disaster.

Income related documents should be next. Copies of your recent pay stubs and contact information for your employer can be useful. If you're self-employed or a business owner, you might want to include a summary of your quarterly earnings or balance sheets.

If you're an investor, include a list of your investments -- annuities, retirement funds such as 401K or IRAs, mutual funds, and other stock portfolios. A quick tip - ensure that you have the contact details of your investment advisor.

Next up - a list of your credit card and banking info. No, don't include your passwords or pin codes! Just information like account numbers, institution name, routing numbers, and contact details of the institutions.

Lastly, consider including a list of utilities and service companies which you need to contact for interruptions or issues post-storm. Think electricity, water, cell phone, Internet, cable, etc.

Now, for the more digital savvy out there, consider storing this info digitally. You can keep everything in a password-protected document on a secure cloud server or a portable hard drive. Think of it as your digital safety deposit box! However, ensure that you follow all best practices for storing sensitive data online to avoid any cyber theft.

Remember, the purpose of the financial emergency kit is to have a one-stop solution for all your crucial financial documents to recover from an emergency more efficiently. No one wants to deal with avoidable financial headaches while rebuilding their lives after a hurricane or any other disaster.

Of course, keep your kit in a water and fire-safe box. Store it in a secure yet easy-to-retrieve location. And finally, maintain it - ensure that the documents are up-to-date, especially insurance policies, and replace them as necessary.

So West Coast Floridians, that's your guide to creating a financial emergency kit. A little preparation can go a long way in helping you weather the storm, or more precisely, the financial aftermath of a hurricane.

Remember, the aim is to build resilience against not just the physical impact of a hurricane, but the financial one too. Remember to think ahead, prepare, and stay safe."

Chapter 7: Community Resources

You're not in this alone, remember that. The west coast of Florida is chock-full of community resources specifically set up to help folks like us out in case of a hurricane. Got your local emergency services--police, firefighters, ambulance--on speed dial? They're there to keep you safe. Then you've got dedicated community support networks and neighborhood plans. Having a grasp on your local neighborhood's hurricane emergency plan can put your mind at ease, knowing that there's a solid cooperative system already in place. What's more, if you've got that fire in your belly and are itching to do more, there's an entire array of volunteer opportunities to chip in. From the Red Cross to community shelters, giving back isn't just about lending a hand. It primes you with skills and first-hand knowledge that could turn out to be life-saving, not just for others, but for you and for your loved ones as well. And don't forget, sometimes the heroes aren't the ones braving the elements, but the friendly voice on the other end of a support hotline. So, when you're prepping for that next hurricane, don't be shy. Reach out, tap into these resources, get to know your community because we're all in this together.

Local Emergency Services

At the heart of our preparation for a hurricane is the understanding that we're not alone in the struggle. Our Local Emergency Services are ready to jump in and offer help when we need it the most. It's vital to be aware of the resources they provide and how to effectively utilize them.

Situated across the west coast of Florida are local fire and rescue departments that play an essential role during a hurricane. These guys don't just put out fires; they're trained in search and rescue missions, medical emergencies, and flood response. Being aware of the nearest fire station and basic contact information could be a lifesaver.

You can't overlook the importance of Emergency Medical Services (EMS). During a hurricane, they're out there, rushing to medical emergencies despite the treacherous weather conditions. If someone in your household or neighborhood requires medical attention during a hurricane, it's indispensable to know their number.

The local police department too provides crucial services during such emergencies. They work round the clock to maintain public safety and order, guarding against potential looting, and assisting in evacuation efforts. Being familiar with your local police department's contact information and location proves beneficial during emergency situations.

Being aware of your local Emergency Management Agency could also come in handy. These professionals coordinate responses to disasters like hurricanes, working with local, state, and federal resources to manage evacuation procedures, provide real-time updates, and put recovery plans into action.

There are also community emergency response teams - often simply known as CERTs. These are groups of trained citizens who offer support and provide immediate assistance within their communities. Having their contact could serve as a useful backup or supplement to other emergency services.

The American Red Cross maintains active branches on Florida's west coast, offering a multitude of resources during a hurricane. They open and manage shelters, provide meals, and have health-services assistance available for residents.

Salvation Army also plays a big part in disaster relief. They have trucks that serve meals and provide disaster relief supplies and long-term recovery help. Knowing their nearest location can be crucial in crisis situations.

The 211 Helpline is often overlooked, but it serves as an important source of information during a disaster. Available 24/7, it provides free and confidential advice on where to find local resources like food, shelter, and mental health support. Always keep this number handy.

For residents with pets, Animal Control services can also be highly valuable. They can provide support if pets go missing or provide resources for pet-friendly shelters. Having their contact information is great if you're a pet owner.

If you or someone in your household relies on home medical equipment or services, you need to know about your local health department. They can provide information and resources, including dialysis sites, oxygen supplies, and more.

Finally, there's the Federal Emergency Management Agency (FEMA). They provide disaster survivor assistance, helping individuals and businesses recover from the loss suffered during a hurricane. They also provide real-time updates and alerts through their app.

One major takeaway here is that preparation is essential! Take the time to gather contact information for these services and keep it both digitally and physically. You never know when you'll need to access it quickly, even if power or mobile networks are down.

Remember, no one has to face a disaster alone. We're fortunate to have a network of local emergency services in Florida that are ready and equipped to respond when we need them. Knowing who they are, what they do, and how to reach them is an invaluable part of your hurricane preparedness strategy.

Don't forget to share this information with your neighbors and community members. The more people who have this information, the better prepared we all can be. Be informed, be prepared, and you'll weather the storm successfully!

Community Support and Neighborhood Plans

The storm is just one part of the hurricane's challenge. An equally important aspect is how the community responds to it. Being part of a tight-knit community can make all the difference in times of crisis. For this reason, knowing your neighbors and networking with local community organizations can be incredibly beneficial. In this section, we'll discuss community support and neighborhood plans to benefit during hurricanes.

Local community organizations often provide immediate support and relief during emergencies, in conjunction with government and national organizations. These can include food, shelter, clothing, and medical care. It's a good idea to familiarize yourself with these groups before a hurricane strikes so you know where to go for help if you need it.

In addition to local organizations, consider initiating or joining a neighborhood emergency preparedness organization. Such groups can coordinate preparation measures, pool resources, and organize assistance to meet the needs of the residents in the aftermath of a hurricane.

One way to catalyze this community initiative is to form a hurricane preparation team within your neighborhood. Together, you can assess collective resources, develop a shared plan, and construct a team of volunteers ready to help when the hurricane hits. A coordinated plan can dramatically reduce damage, provide more effective relief and a swift recovery in the aftermath of a hurricane.

Creating a map of your neighborhood detailing routes to local emergency centers and shelters can also be hugely beneficial. This map should be comprehensive, indicating key landmarks and potential obstacles that might be faced in the aftermath of a storm. Distribute copies of this map to your neighbors and members of your local community organizations, ensuring everyone knows the best route to safety.

Setting up a neighborhood communication plan is another essential component of community preparedness. This could be a simple phone tree with contact information, a group chat in a communication app, or a broadcast email list. The point is to have a simple and effective way to disseminate crucial information quickly.

Beyond these basic frameworks, community coordination could extend to shared provisioning and storage, of supplies like water, food, medical kits, generators, and more. For instance, certain neighbors with secure, higher ground homes could volunteer to store part of the communal water supply.

Indeed, pooling resources can make a significant difference in preparedness. Not everyone will be able to afford a generator for power outages, but perhaps one could be purchased collectively by the community, ensuring vital things like power for medical equipment or refrigeration can be preserved.

In the spirit of coordination and organization, skill exchange and training within the community could be a valuable initiative. Those with medical training, experience in construction, or people with survival skills could give brief workshops to equip others with specific skills in hurricane preparation, endurance, and recovery.

The support that community and neighborhood plans offer is not limited to the tangible, immediate advantages. It also creates a sense of togetherness, teamwork, and neighborliness that can be a source of emotional and psychological strength during difficult times.

While professional emergency services are vital, neighborhood and zoning councils can provide a more immediate and localized response. Establishing a working relationship with your local council can often provide access to resources and coordination you might miss otherwise.

Finally, remember that effective community support and neighborhood plans are not about a single individual striving to save the day. The goal is a community effort that supports all members regardless of their capabilities, age, health status, or resources. This collaborative approach can not only weather a hurricane but build stronger, more interconnected, and resilient communities that will thrive long after the storm has passed.

With the tips and strategies outlined in this chapter, the power of community support is at your fingertips. As you prepare for hurricane season, keep in mind this maxim: alone we can do so little, together we can do so much.

Remember, knowledge is power and preparation is the key to survival. It's not a matter of if, but when the next hurricane will hit Florida's west coast. With a solid neighborhood plan and a supportive community in place, you'll be ready to face it when it comes.

Volunteer Opportunities

Helping your neighbors and the wider community can be a rewarding experience, especially in the aftermath of a hurricane. We are stronger together. And sacrificially giving your time and energy in assisting others unearths just how strong these bonds can be. In West Florida, there are several volunteer opportunities available that involve various stages of hurricane preparedness and response.

The American Red Cross, for instance, depends heavily on the goodwill of community members when responding to natural disasters. This widely recognized organization recruits volunteers to assist in distributing emergency supplies, providing first aid, and offering emotional support to victims of hurricanes. They also offer training sessions in disaster response which can equip you with practical skills and provide invaluable experience.

In addition to the Red Cross, the Salvation Army also has a robust volunteer system. They play a significant role in emergency situations, providing food, shelter, and support to those affected during difficult times. The Salvation Army's Emergency Disaster Services is always on the lookout for willing hands to help in recovery efforts. From cooking and serving meals to cleaning up debris, there's a task suited to everyone's abilities.

Local food banks are another great place to volunteer. In the wake of a hurricane, many families may find themselves in need of basic supplies. The Feeding Florida – including Food Bank of Manatee and Feeding Tampa Bay – help address this need and are always in need of help. Volunteers can help with sorting, packing, and distributing supplies to affected families.

Disaster response isn't the only area where volunteers are needed, however. Preparation is key when it comes to minimizing the impact of hurricanes, and there are organizations geared towards this. One of these is Habitat for Humanity. This organization often hosts events where volunteers can help build or fortify homes, ensuring they can withstand the onslaught of a hurricane. This work often takes place well before hurricane season and provides a measure of peace and security to families in vulnerable areas.

The United Way's 'Mission United' program is another initiative where pre-hurricane volunteering is needed. This program is focused on ensuring veterans are well prepared for natural disasters. This includes assembling disaster preparedness kits, as well as providing veterans with training on evacuation and disaster plans.

You may also wish to consider volunteering with a pet rescue organization. With many families forced to evacuate their homes during hurricanes, pets occasionally get left behind. Volunteers with organizations such as the ASPCA and Animal Defense League of Florida are needed to help rescue and shelter these helpless animals. Training is provided to ensure the safety of both volunteers and animals.

If you feel more comfortable volunteering your expertise, consider joining the Florida Crisis Response Team. This group, made up of mental health professionals, offers crucial emotional and psychological support to victims of natural disasters. If you're not a professional but still wish to help, they offer training to lay responders as well.

Emergency Radio Communications is yet another specialized volunteering opportunity. If you have a background in amateur radio or willing to learn, this could be the avenue for you. Amateur radio operators can play a vital role in providing communication assistance during a disaster. Florida's Amateur Radio Emergency Services offers training and guidance throughout the year, providing you with the skills necessary for this critical role.

In addition to these established organizations, there are also informal volunteering opportunities that surface during times of crisis. Community groups often form ad hoc distribution centers, offering food, water, clothing, and other necessities. These pop-up aid stations are generally community-born efforts and involve neighbors helping neighbors, making them an effective and personal way to help out.

Finally, volunteering doesn't always mean physical labor. If you're unable to participate in physical tasks, consider volunteering your time digitally - sharing useful information, coordinating aid, and spreading awareness on social media. This kind of information distribution is crucial during crises and can be performed from the safety of your home.

Regardless of where you decide to lend your time, it's important to remember, volunteering is as much about community building as it is about disaster response and preparedness. The connections you forge and the shared experiences can foster a sense of belonging and camaraderie that extends far beyond the hurricane season.

Remember, volunteers are a vital part of a successful disaster response operation. Teams turn the tide in moments of crisis and can provide a sense of hope and support to those who are affected. In volunteering, you're not just giving of your time and effort – you're giving a measure of relief, hope, and reassurance to those impacted by these storms, making you a real-life superhero in their hurricane survival story.

And remember, these organizations largely depend on generous individuals offering their assistance. Whatever skills, talents, or time you possess, there's likely a place for you in the world of hurricane preparedness and response volunteerism. It's indeed all hands on deck when a hurricane hits, and every contribution, no matter how small, can make a big difference. Explore these opportunities, connect with organizations, and find the best way you can help your community.

Chapter 8: Special Considerations

Let's switch gears a bit and talk about our particularly vulnerable folks — kids, seniors, disabled individuals, and yep, even our fluffy friends that walk, fly, buzz, or slither. For families with kids, think of fun but educational games to help them understand the importance of hurricane protocols and emergency drills. Now, for the seniors or those with disabilities, you'll want to ensure that their essentials, such as medications and healthcare devices, are ready and easy to carry. And these folks may need additional help during evacuation or when hunkering down. You got to be ready for that. Don't forget our pet buddies, too! Make sure you've got pet-friendly shelters in mind, or prepared at home. And their emergency kit? It should have food, water, a leash for dogs, a carrier for cats, and a picture of your pet (in case they run off in a panic). For livestock owners, early evacuation is key and always have your vet's number handy. It's a part of life here on the west coast of Florida that hurricanes can cause a ruckus, but with some extra thought, everyone we care about can be kept safe.

Families with Children

Hurricane preparedness for families with children demands a bit more attention. The overall safety of your kiddos is the number one priority. Let's explore some ideas to keep them safe and somewhat thrilled through this hide-and-seek with Mother Nature.

When preparing for a hurricane, start off by making sure the kids understand what's about to happen. Explain hurricanes in a simplistic, non-scary tone. You don't want to frighten them; you just want them to understand that they need to cooperate and why. A family meeting can do wonders, where you casually chat about hurricanes, how they work, and what are the dos and don'ts.

Next, kids need structure. Try establishing routines and keeping them as close to normal as possible. For instance, if there's a nightly story time, keep that going. If your kid looks forward to pancakes on Friday mornings, strive to make that happen, even if it's with the help of a gas stove after a power outage. Don't underestimate the comforting power of a routine in a stressful situation.

Talk to them about the family's evacuation plan. Clarity is key. Educate them on the evacuation route, the emergency contacts, and the safe places in the house. Make sure they know the importance of staying together as a family during the ordeal.

Now, let's look at supplies and how they differ when children are involved. Apart from the basics like food, water, flashlights, first aid kit - you also want to pack some comfort items. This can be a favorite toy, a picture book, some craft supplies, or anything else that could help distract or comfort your children during this time.

Loading up on child-specific supplies is also crucial. If you have a baby, that means diapers, baby food, bottles, and formula. For children with specific dietary requirements, account for that in your emergency food supply. The same goes if your child has any medical conditions or needs special medication; stock up on that ahead of time.

Keeping children occupied during a hurricane is another thing you have to plan for. Gather a collection of board games, activity books, or any handheld electronic games to keep them engaged and distracted. Remember, bored kids can become anxious or cranky kids.

Remember to talk about the hurricane in an ongoing way. Their curiosity might lead them to ask many questions; take the time to answer these patiently. If they show fear or anxiety, reassure them that as a family, you will get through this together.

Throughout the storm, be a great model of calm and control. Children look to adults for cues on how to behave. If they see you panicking, stress is likely to kick in. But if you're steady-as-she-goes, they'll be far more likely to stay calm too.

After the hurricane, let them be part of the 'recovery phase', based on their age and abilities. Allowing them to help in manageable tasks can provide a sense of control and accomplishment in a potentially chaotic situation. This might include cleaning up their toys, helping to sort laundry, or packing away emergency supplies.

If your home has been critically damaged by the hurricane and you seek temporary shelter elsewhere, be sure to maintain open and consistent communication with your children. Little bits of normalcy, like sticking to bedtimes and maintaining family meals, can offer comfort amid displacement.

Lastly, pay attention to how your children are processing the events. Some kids cope well, while others may have a harder time and show signs of stress, fear or anxiety. If needed, don't hesitate to seek professional help. Services and support are available to help kids navigate through the emotional aftermath of a disaster.

The real trick to navigating a hurricane with children in the fold is to remain flexible. Your plan may change a thousand times based on the circumstances, but that's okay. The goal is to keep the children safe, well-fed, and comforted, and with the right planning, you can ensure you're up to the task.

Next, we'll explore how to prepare the elderly and disabled individuals tirelessly, considering their unique needs. But that's a story for another chapter. For now, take this information, digest it, and begin working on that family plan. There's always a silver lining through every storm cloud; let's ensure the journey is safe and manageable for your precious little ones.

Senior Citizens and Disabled Individuals

As we turn our attention to special considerations in hurricane preparedness, let's dive into what senior citizens and disabled individuals should keep in mind. With the aging population and an increase in the number of individuals with disabilities, addressing the needs of these groups during a hurricane is critical.

Severe weather disrupts lives and even a well-prepared individual can find it challenging. For elderly citizens and individuals with special needs, hurricanes pose unique problems. Physical limitations, medical conditions and increased reliance on public services can be a complex mix when preparing for or surviving a storm.

It's vital to start planning well ahead of hurricane season. A 'just in time' approach is a poor companion here. Think about the potential challenges and come up with practical solutions. If mobility is an issue, think about strategies to aid in evacuation or secure safe spaces within your home. If you rely on medication or medical equipment, make sure there's an ample supply and that your equipment can function without electricity.

Arrange a support network - family, friends, neighbors or local community organizations - that understands your specific needs. Grabbing a bit of help from those around you can go a long way. Share your emergency plan with this network and make sure they know what medications and equipment you rely on.

Formulating an evacuation plan is crucial for senior citizens and disabled individuals. Every second counts during an evacuation, and a clear and easy-to-follow plan will ensure a fast and smooth exit. If you're wheelchair-bound or have difficulty traveling, plan for accessible transportation and evacuation routes.

Being unable to communicate or express oneself during emergencies can also be terrifying. Make sure you have several methods of communication in hand. Whether it's a whistle, phone, or a communication board, ensure you can convey your needs in an emergency.

In case of evacuation, temporary shelter isn't always equipped with what you need. It's essential to pack an emergency kit customized to your requirements. This could include items such as spare batteries for hearing aids, medicines, extra glasses, copies of prescriptions, oxygen, wheelchair batteries, food for special diets, supplies for service animals, etc.

If you require electricity for medical devices or refrigeration for medication, plan for power outages. Portable coolers and back-up power sources like a generator or battery pack can be life-saving in these situations.

Sometimes, staying home isn't the safest choice. Look into local emergency shelters ahead of time and find out if they meet your needs. Some communities have Special Needs Shelters designed to cater to those with medical issues. Registration is usually required, so don't delay this!

And don't forget to keep all important documents safe and accessible. These include insurance policies, medical records, and legal documents. You might consider creating digital copies and storing them securely online for easy access.

After a hurricane, recovery can be even more difficult for senior citizens and individuals with disabilities. Rely on your network, utilize local resources, and don't be afraid to ask for help. Familiarize yourself with available services from FEMA, Red Cross and other community organizations. They can provide assistance with cleanup, housing and even mental health support.

Bear in mind, hurricanes are stressful events and can exacerbate existing health problems. It's important to manage stress levels and maintain a routine where possible. Link with mental health professionals, keep medications in check, and maintain your usual diet to cope with the stress better.

Preparing for a hurricane requires thought, planning, and action. When we consider the needs of seniors and people with disabilities, it requires a bit more elbow grease. Never underestimate the importance of planning, networking, and informing yourself of the available resources to help weather the storm.

In the end, the key takeaway is this: everyone deserves to feel secure during unsteady times. By thinking proactively and putting precautionary measures in place, senior citizens and disabled individuals can weather the storm just as well as anyone.

Care for Pets and Livestock

In the hustle and bustle of preparing for a hurricane, it's vital not to forget about our four-legged friends and feathered companions. These family members will also be heavily affected by a hurricane and require just as much attention and care as your human household.

Pets and livestock depend solely on their owners for their safety and survival. In the face of destructive weather patterns, not all survival procedures are suitable for humans and animals alike. Let's figure out how to get 'em through the storm safe and sound.

First off, it's critical to find out if your area is prone to mandatory evacuations. If it is, you'll need to look up pet-friendly shelters beforehand. It's a bum deal, but not all places will accept pets. Check in with local animal shelters, friends, family, or pet-friendly hotels outside the evacuation zone where you can take your pets.

For those with livestock, evacuation may not always be possible due to the size and quantity of the animals. In such cases, the best bet is to identify a higher ground area on your property, where livestock can stay safe from flood waters. Be sure to move food, water, and supplies there as well.

Don't forget to pack a pet emergency kit. This kit should include food, water, leashes, toys, beds, litter boxes, and any meds your furry friend might need. Also, it's wise to throw in vet records and recent photos in case you're separated during the chaos.

Pro tip: To minimize stress for your pet, try to keep their feeding and exercise routines consistent. A familiar routine can go a long way in providing some comfort in an unfamiliar environment or situation.

Microchipping your pets can be a real life-saver in a hurricane. They can run scared during a storm, and collars can slip off. Microchips provide a reliable way for rescuers to identify and contact pet owners. Make sure to register your contact details and keep them updated.

Just like for humans, it's important to have a plan for post-storm recovery for pets and livestock. Flooding, downed power lines, and scattered debris can create a hazardous environment. After the storm, only allow pets and livestock out when it's safe, and continue to give them good, clean water and food.

When you're examining livestock after a storm, look out for any wounds, lameness, or signs of discomfort. If you find anything concerning, don't try to wing it; consult a veterinarian right away.

Storms can be downright scary for our pets, causing them to act out of the ordinary. If you notice your pet behaving differently after the storm, it may be a reaction to the stress. There's a chance they might hide, become more clingy, or even become aggressive. Understanding and patience go a long way until they feel safe again.

While dogs and cats are the most common pets affected during hurricanes, don't forget about the little critters like hamsters, fish, and birds. These creatures need equal attention and special care. For example, a fish tank's water needs extra aeration if there's a power outage, and smaller pets need warm and secure carriers.

Just remember folks, caring for pets and livestock before, during, and after a hurricane isn't an optional job for pet owners — it's a responsibility. Plan ahead, stay alert and remember, the comfort and familiar presence of pet owners can ease a pet's stress significantly during such events.

A hurricane can be a stressful experience, but by including your pets and livestock in your safety plans, they can weather the storm alongside you. Life on the west coast of Florida is full of sunshine most days, but when those hurricanes hit, our whole community needs to stand together. That includes our animals, big and small.

In the end, right, it's described best by saying: preparing for your pets or livestock during a hurricane is just as important as preparing for your human family. If you do this right, you'll get through it all, with all family members safely by your side.

Chapter 9: Post-Storm Recovery

Once the winds die down and the all-clear is given, the real work begins. Starting with a safe and cautious assessment of the damage will help you identify potential hazards, like downed power lines or unstable structures. Snap photos for documentation - they'll come in handy when dealing with insurance and authorities. Speaking of which, don't delay in reaching out to them; the quicker you file a claim or report, the better. As far as cleanup and rebuilding go, plan for it to be a marathon, not a sprint. Take it step-by-step, prioritize vital repairs, and don't be afraid to ask for help. The community often pulls together in the aftermath of these storms, so pool resources when you can. Finally, don't discount the psychological impact of a hurricane. They can be traumatic, especially for the young or elderly. Talk about the experience; support networks - both formal and informal - can be a big help. In the wake of a storm, remember: you're not alone and help can be found in the most surprising places.

Assessing Damage Safely

After a hurricane, the debris-laden home front might represent a war zone more than the haven you left. Whispering palms might groan under the weight of packed wind debris and streets can turn into channels. It's a shock and one's first instinct may be to jump right in to clear and ascertain damage. However, safety should always remain the top priority.

Unlike in action movies, when you charge into a building post-disaster, you're risking far more than a twist of drama. Damage, from subtle to significant, can turn your abode into a nest of hazards - unstable structures, hidden sharp objects, exposed wiring and more. Sometimes, unexploded ordnance from World War II turns up on Florida's beaches after a storm, true story! Here's how you can mitigate the risks:

Wear Appropriate Clothing: Before a walk-through of your residence or any affected property, dressing for the occasion is crucial. Think sturdy boots, a long-sleeved shirt, gloves, and protective eyewear. Forget about keeping time with fashion, this is about safety. The idea is to protect yourself from sharp objects, infected water, and creatures that might have taken shelter in your rubble.

Watch Where You're Stepping: Flooded areas or rooms might have hidden threats, like fallen, invisible wires, glass shards or nails. Use a long stick to probe the area in front of you before stepping in. Imagine yourself as a wary adventurer, tentatively exploring an unknown terrain.

Structural integrity: Be aware of sagging roofs, unstable walls or floors, damaged beams and pillars. Any signs of instability warrant a safe distance and a call to appropriate professionals who can accurately evaluate the extend of the damage. Sounds of shifting or cracking could also indicate unstable structures, so keep those ears open!

Electrical Hazards: One of the top culprits of post-hurricane injuries is electrocution from downed power lines or submerged outlets. Simply put, water and electricity don't mix. Make sure the power is turned off before you return home. Better yet, have a qualified electrician to clear your home of any electrical hazards.

Gas Leaks: Smell rotten eggs? It might not be that half-eaten sandwich you left before evacuating but a gas leak. Contact your gas company or a licensed professional to assess the situation. The last thing you want after surviving a hurricane is to have your house explode.

Water Damage: Flood water can wreak havoc on homes, but it could also hide many dangers like snakes, debris and.It can also lead to mold growth if it remains stagnant for a long period. Ensure all water is extracted and your home thoroughly dried to prevent these issues.

Inhabitants: In Florida, all manner of creatures could have made your home theirs during the storm. Everything from snakes, spiders, to rats and alligators might now call your personal quarters, home. Call animal control or a professional cleanup crew to handle wildlife invasions. In the meantime, keep a safe distance.

Sharp Objects: Look out for broken glass, nails, wire, or any other sharp objects. Bits and pieces from shattered windows or fallen rooftops might be strewn about. Always wear gloves and sturdy shoes for protection. As much as you want to recover from this crisis quickly, a trip to the ER is something you'd want to avoid.

Falling Items: Okay, so the walls are stable. But what about that antique chandelier precariously hanging by a thread? Or the cabinet sagging under the weight of water-logged books? Take note of things that could fall and cause injuries.

After you have assessed the situation, document it meticulously for insurance and restoration purposes. Take photographs, note down details of all damaged items and areas, and retain any receipts for repair work done. This will be of great help when filing your insurance claim.

Mind you, all this advice is not to scare you, but to prepare you. Now that you're equipped with these safety tips, you'll be ready when the time comes to step into the aftermath of a storm and handle it like a pro.

While our natural tendency is towards swift recovery, the strategy should be smart recovery. Doing things the right way can save a lot of headaches down the line – not to mention keeping you and your loved ones safe.

While facing such damage can undoubtedly be overwhelming, remember this — homes can be rebuilt, possessions can be replaced, but you're unique and irreplaceable. So take the time, approach this with caution, and stay safe!

Contacting Insurance and Authorities

After the storm has passed, you're bound to be a bundle of nerves. Everyone's anxious to assess the damage and get started on the road to recovery. Before you begin that phase, it's essential to get in touch with key parties - first, your insurance company, and then, local authorities. Let's break those down.

Alert Your Insurance Company

First things first, loop in your insurance provider. Actually, strike that - even before that, be sure you're safe. Only after confirming your safety and those around you, reach out to your insurance agent. The sooner they're informed, the quicker they can start the claims process.

It's critical not to underestimate or underreport your property damage. As the saying goes, the devil's in the details - that's true here too. Make sure you're thorough. If it's feasible, click pictures and record videos of the damage. That can be invaluable evidence when you're bargaining with insurance adjusters.

You might have multiple policies - homeowner's, flood, windstorm. So, you'll possibly need to make multiple calls. Sure, it's a pain, but hey, that's why we prepare in advance, right? Keep all essential documents organized and in hand for these conversations.

Cooperating with Adjusters

Once you've lodged your claim, your insurance company will assign an adjuster to evaluate the damage. Cooperate with them. They're not the bad guys. Their job is to assess the situation objectively and determine your entitlement under the policy.

Remember those photographs and videos you took? Show them to the adjuster, especially if your property has undergone some cleaning or repairs since the incident. This evidence can aid the adjuster in his assessment and help secure proper compensation for you.

Reach Out to Local Authorities

Once the initial commotion has subsided and your insurance claims are underway, it's time to turn to local authorities. Contact your city or county's emergency management office or disaster assistance agency. They'll guide you on the necessary steps to take in the aftermath of the storm, like getting a disaster housing or assistance loan, for instance.

These local agencies are typically flooded with calls and queries immediately following a hurricane. If you're safe and relatively sound, it might be helpful to hold off on calling straight away. Give them time to handle the most pressing situations.

Contacting Health Authorities

Don't hesitate to contact health authorities if necessary. Families with senior citizens or individuals with special needs might need immediate medical support or replenishing crucial medicinal supplies post-hurricane. It's important to know your local health department's contact information even before a disaster strikes.

Reach out to Utility Companies

In the aftermath of a storm, it's likely that your home has lost essential utilities like electricity, gas, and water. It's crucial to contact your utility providers as soon as possible to report outages or damages and learn about their recovery efforts.

Keep a list of all necessary emergency numbers – including those of your utility companies – handy. It's always better to be well-informed and prepared before disaster strikes than panic in its wake.

To wrap things up, immediately after a storm, keep your wits about you. Be proactive, but also patient. Contact your insurance provider and necessary authorities in a timely manner, but remember, they too are likely swamped with requests and inquiries. Doing your part to stay informed, organized, and calm can make a world of difference.

The world might look a little topsy-turvy right after a hurricane, but knowing who to contact and how to navigate the process can at least get the ball rolling toward normalcy.

Cleanup and Rebuilding

When the storm has passed, and it's safe to venture outside, the cleanup and rebuilding process begins. It can be a long and challenging task, but with the right guidance, you can make it through with relative ease.

Cleanup after a hurricane isn't as simple as picking up trash or clearing a driveway. Pathways may be blocked by fallen trees, power lines may be down, and in some cases, buildings may have collapsed. It's these situations where you have to be cautious and meticulous in your approach.

The first thing to do is to assess any damage that may have been inflicted upon your property. Walk around and take note of any flooded areas, damaged buildings, or dangerous obstacles. Once this is done, the cleanup process can begin in earnest.

During cleanup, remember to prioritize safety. Always wear sturdy shoes to protect your feet from debris and always wear gloves when picking up any objects. If you suspect structural damage to your home, do not attempt to enter until a professional has deemed it safe. It is better to be safe than sorry when dealing with the aftermath of a hurricane.

Once preliminary safety checks are done, it's time to start the clean-up. Clearing debris can be a daunting chore. Torn branches, broken glass, and other shattered items will need to be picked up and disposed of properly. Disposal services are usually overwhelmed after a hurricane, so it might be good to secure a rental dumpster ahead of time.

Always remember to document any damages you discover thoroughly before cleanup begins. Take photos and detailed notes. This documentation will be essential when filing insurance claims later on. Also, be aware that the removal of certain items might require professional help. This includes fallen trees, damaged vehicles, and large pieces of a collapsed structure.

With the majority of the debris cleared, the focus can now shift to rebuilding and repairing. This task can feel overwhelming at first, but having a plan can help make the process much more manageable.

Depending upon the severity of the damage to your home, you may need to seek temporary housing while repairs take place. Reach out to neighbors, friends, and family if you can. There are also disaster relief organizations that offer shelter and assistance to those displaced by the hurricane.

Repairs should begin with the most crucial parts of your house. This often includes patching up any holes in the roof, fixing broken windows, and patching up damaged walls. These tasks might require a skilled professional, so don't hesitate to hire one if needed.

Sometimes, the damage can be far-reaching and beyond your control. If the hurricane has swept away large portions of your home, or if there is substantial structural damage, there may be no choice but to seek professional assistance for demolition and reconstruction. Homeowners insurance may cover this but always check with your provider before making any decisions.

As the rebuilding process takes place, ensure to include better protection methods from possible future hurricanes. This could be anything from installing hurricane shutters on your windows, strengthening your roof, or even raising your home above flood levels. Investing in such protections can pay off hugely in the long run.

If you're a part of a community or a neighborhood association, see if they're coordinating any efforts for cleanup and rebuilding. Working together as a community can make the process easier and more efficient for everyone involved. Besides, the support of a community can significantly ease the emotional burden of recovery.

Lastly, it's crucial to take care of yourself during this time. Dealing with the aftermath of a hurricane can be emotionally challenging, adding stress and anxiety to an already difficult situation. Don't hesitate to reach out to mental health resources to help process the event and pave the way for recovery.

In conclusion, the recovery process after a hurricane can be a long journey filled with challenges. But by taking it one step at a time, focusing on safety, and taking proper precautions, you can navigate through the cleanup and rebuilding phase successfully. Remember, the important part isn't how quickly everything gets back to normal. It's ensuring safety and the proper reconstruction of your home for future security and peace of mind.

Coping with Psychological Effects

Once the storm passes, there's a collective sigh of relief, but often, the emotional trauma persists. Hurricanes bring with them more than physical damage; they can wreak havoc on our mental health. It's important to understand how to cope with the psychological impacts of these events.

The chaos and unpredictability of a hurricane can lead to stress and anxiety, both during and after the event. You might feel on edge, have trouble sleeping, or even experience nightmares about the event. These reactions are perfectly normal and are your body's way of processing trauma.

The key is not to suppress these feelings. It's okay to feel upset, scared, or anxious. Pushing those feelings away won't help. Instead, let yourself feel and accept these emotions. Validate your emotions and understand that it's alright to feel this way.

But don't dwell in this space for too long. Give yourself some time to adjust and then start focusing on putting the pieces back together. Adopting an action-oriented approach can help alleviate feelings of anxiety and distress since it provides a practical outlet for your energy.

Communicating about your experiences can also be therapeutic. Talk to someone you trust about your fears and concerns. Share what you went through. This can provide a sense of relief and reduce feelings of isolation. Remember, many others are also going through the same experience.

Exercise can be an essential tool for managing stress and anxiety. If possible, engage in physical activity like walks or yoga to help reduce feelings of tension. But remember to do what feels right for you: pushing yourself too hard when you're feeling emotionally drained can add to your stress levels rather than reducing it.

Sometimes, you might need professional help to deal with the emotional aftermath of a hurricane. If you're feeling persistently anxious, depressed, or disturbed, consider seeking support from a mental health professional. Various community resources often offer counseling services after a natural disaster. You should not feel ashamed or embarrassed to seek help. This is an extraordinary circumstance, and it's okay to reach out for support.

Helping others can also provide an emotional boost. If you're physically able, volunteering for clean-up efforts or other community services can give you a sense of purpose and control. It's a tangible way of working towards recovery, and it also fosters a sense of community solidarity.

For kids, hurricanes can be particularly traumatic. As a caregiver, reassure them about their safety and explain the situation appropriately. Encourage them to express their feelings through activities like drawing or story-telling. Provide a stable environment as much as possible, as regular routines can offer a sense of normality amid chaos.

Unplugging from non-stop news coverage can also help manage your psychological well-being. While it's important to stay informed about recovery efforts and important updates, constantly watching or hearing about devastation can add to your stress and anxiety. Designate specific times to check in with news updates, but otherwise, try to engage in positive and constructive activities instead.

Finally, remember that healing takes time. Coping with the psychological effects of a hurricane does not happen overnight. It's a process, and it's different for everyone. Don't rush yourself or others. Take one step at a time on the road to recovery.

Nurturing your mental health is as important as restoring your physical surroundings in the aftermath of a hurricane. Building resilience is not just about planning for the physical impact of disasters; it's about coping with emotional aftermath too. And just as we prepare for hurricanes physically, it's just as crucial to equip ourselves mentally.

West coast of Florida, we've shown our resilience before, and we'll do so again. Let's take care of each other, be patient with ourselves, and remember – it's okay to ask for help.

Chapter 10: Lessons from the Past

Looking back at West Florida's hurricane history, there's a gold mine of insight to be gleaned. Each storm has brought along its unique set of challenges, and in handling them, we've armed ourselves with lessons that form a critical part of our preparedness plans today. Take Hurricane Donna, for instance. Hitting the west coast of Florida back in 1960, it taught us the importance of staying informed. Through the uncertainty and unpredictability of the storm, access to reliable and accurate information was paramount in making decisions that saved lives. Then there was the devastation caused by Hurricane Charley in 2004 — a stark reminder that structural integrity isn't just about roofs and windows — it's about strengthening our community ties and pooling our resources for the collective survival of our neighborhoods. Likewise, Hurricane Irma showed us the significance of evaluating the avant-garde techniques that predict a hurricane's path with its unexpected shift. The constant across all these hurricanes isn't just the destruction, but the resilience that it bred. These lessons should ignite a fire in us to always stay proactive — a beacon to prepare, counter, and rebuild even when the skies are crystal clear. Through understanding our past, we can build a future that's better braced for these coastal curveballs.

Case Studies: West Florida Hurricanes

The west coast of Florida, known for its stunning sunsets and balmy breezes, has also been the stage of numerous hurricanes. These intense storms, fueled by the heat of tropical waters, have shaped the landscape and the lives of Floridians. Here, we'll dive into some significant hurricanes that left indelible marks on West Florida and offer takeaways from these events.

Let's start with Hurricane Donna that struck in 1960. Often referred to as one of the all-time great Atlantic hurricanes, Donna left a path of destruction that residents are unlikely to forget. With wind speeds roaring at 130 miles per hour, Donna caused significant damage to property along Florida's west coast. Yet, it was the storm surge, peaking at a staggering 13 feet in many areas, which proved most destructive. Concerningly, residents were ill-prepared for such a powerful surge. The aftermath provided a stark lesson on the importance of understanding storm surge risks and preparing accordingly.

A slightly more recent example is Hurricane Charley, a compact but furious cyclone that struck in 2004. With a size smaller than average hurricanes but packing an impressive Category 4 punch, Charley taught the world that size isn't necessarily an indicator of a storm's destructive capacity. The people of Punta Gorda and Port Charlotte could tell you about the devastation and loss, the damage to homes and businesses. From this, it's clear that assumptions about a storm's power based solely on size can be misleading and dangerous.

Fast forward to 2017 when Hurricane Irma hit the west coast of Florida. Although expecting it to land on the east coast initially, Irma took an unexpected turn, catching many off guard. With this, we're reminded that hurricane paths can be unpredictable and that all coastal regions should prepare regardless of forecasted projections. Even areas thought to be safe can't afford to rest on their laurels.

When Hurricanes Hermine and Michael hit the Panhandle region, they brought with them the harsh reminder that intense storms can and will reach this often-overlooked region. With preparations often focused on the state's southern tip and central regions, residents in this area were caught flat-footed. The importance of dispelling this regional complacency cannot be overstated.

In 2005, with Hurricane Wilma, Floridians got a grim warning about the severe effects of back-to-back hurricanes. Coming on the heels of Katrina and Rita, Wilma was the exclamation point on an already disastrous hurricane season. Widespread damage, compounded by the lingering effects of previous storms, hammered home the brutal reality of multi-hit seasons. Preparations must account for the potential impact of several storms in one season.

Finally, a look at the destructive Hurricane Andrew of 1992 serves as a potent reminder of the potential for extreme hurricane events. Andrew's 165-mile-per-hour winds and monstrous storm surge flattened large parts of Florida's east coast. It's sensible here to note that such violent storms are not confined to the east coast alone, and west coast residents should be prepared for hurricanes of equal magnitude.

While these examples paint a harrowing picture, it's crucial to remember they also represent opportunities for learning and growth. Each hurricane brings with it lessons, mostly hard-earned, that can be used to better prepare for future storms and hopefully limit their impacts.

The essential takeaway here is that hurricanes don't discriminate. They can and will hit anywhere along Florida's coastline. Being underprepared or dismissing a storm because it appears small or is heading for another area can be a dangerous gamble.

We also learn that we need preparations suited for multiple hits. Sometimes, storms come in quick succession, leaving scarce time for damage control or resource replenishment. Plans should therefore accommodate the possibility of successive hurricanes in a single season.

Additionally, cultivating community resilience is key. Strong community bonds forged through preparedness efforts can make the recovery easier. When disaster strikes, neighbors often become an immediate support system, providing physical aid and emotional support.

Lastly, do not disregard the physical, financial, and psychological toll of surviving a hurricane. Preparation includes acknowledging and planning for these effects, and effectively navigating the recovery period is equally critical.

In West Florida, hurricanes are a part of life. There's something both humbling and empowering in facing these mighty storms. By understanding the risks, arming ourselves with knowledge, preparing thoughtfully, and cultivating resilient communities, we transform our fear into readiness. Through this lens, each hurricane is not merely a destructive force but an opportunity to emerge stronger, more resilient, and more united.

As we move forward, let's keep the lessons of the past close at hand. After all, they form the bedrock of our future preparedness, helping us safeguard our homes, our lives, and our beautiful sun-kissed coast.

Lessons Learned and Future Outlook

As we look back on the history of hurricanes impacting West Florida, there are valuable lessons to be learned. Each storm has given us insights into what works well in our preparations, what needs improvement, and how we can better brace ourselves for future hurricanes.

One of the most significant takeaways is the importance of early preparation. We've learned that waiting until the warning flags go up often results in chaos, stress and inadequate readiness. The successful acquisition of essential supplies and tools, and the construction of secure, safe areas in homes are measures that cannot be efficiently executed in the eleventh hour.

While we've made strides in our physical preparedness methods, the psychological impact of hurricanes on community members can't be overlooked. Support systems to cope with the mental stress and trauma post-hurricane have become a crucially important component of recovery. Future solutions should include more focused attention on outlets for emotional restoration and resilience.

Communication, we've found, is another vital puzzle piece. Whether it's accurate updates about the storm's path, evacuation orders, or providing information about emergency resources, clear and concise communication saves lives. Technological improvements have given us better platforms for sharing information, but it's necessary we continue leveraging these advancements for widespread and timely messaging.

The increased involvement of community members in volunteer opportunities and emergency response initiatives has also been noted. This growing network of trained, knowledgeable helpers has proven invaluable time and again. Future outlook suggests the continued expansion of these initiatives with an emphasis on more training and recruitment drives.

On the flip side, we've identified areas that need improvement. Despite several public awareness initiatives, there still exists a noticeable gap in the general public's understanding of hurricanes. The severity of the different categories of hurricanes and their potential for destruction isn't fully grasped by many. Future efforts should focus on educating residents better, helping them understand the risk and the practical steps they can take for preparedness.

We've also noted that the differences in needs and abilities among various populations like children, seniors, the disabled and pets aren't always adequately addressed in disaster plans. In the future, we must ensure that disaster response systems are inclusive and provide specific support for all these groups.

Financial and legal preparedness is another area where there's room for improvement. A lack of understanding of insurance policies, deficient safeguarding of important documents, and failure to plan for the financial impact of a hurricane are issues that persist. The path forward should include methods for tackling these issues more effectively.

It's evident that climate change is influencing the intensity and frequency of hurricanes. As we look towards the future, this factor must be factored into our hurricane readiness plans. Anticipating more potent storms should guide the strengthening of infrastructure, modifications to building codes, and the planning of evacuation routes.

Moving forward, government agencies, community groups, and individuals must work cohesively to improve hurricane preparedness and response. Only with a collective effort can we reduce the impact of these devastating storms on our neighborhoods and our lives.

Collaborative innovation is key in addressing challenges. The sharing of ideas and solutions between different cities, states, and countries dealing with similar issues can help us continually refine our strategies and approaches.

On the technological front, we're bound to see more innovations that will help us predict, prepare for and recover from hurricanes. Drones for damage assessment, progressive amendment of Alerting system, virtual reality for training purposes – the possibilities are endless and exciting.

Finally, in the face of these powerful natural disasters, a spirit of resilience and community is our greatest ally. Time and again, the people of West Florida have shown extraordinary strength, support, and determination in the aftermath of hurricanes. This is a testament to the power of community – a resource more precious than any material possession.

In conclusion, our past encounters with hurricanes have shaped how we prepare for, handle, and recover from these natural disasters. As we look to the future, let's remember these lessons, continually evolve our strategies, and strive for a safer and more resilient West Florida community.

Appendix A: Emergency Supplies Checklist

Basic Supplies

- **Water:** At least 1 gallon per person per day for at least 3 days

- **Food:** At least a 3-day supply of non-perishable food per person

- **Battery-powered or hand-crank radio** (with NOAA Weather Radio band if possible)

- Flashlight

- First aid kit

- **Extra batteries** (variety of sizes to suit all equipment)

- **Multipurpose tool** (like a Swiss Army knife)

- **Cell phone** with chargers and a backup battery

- **Cash** and change

- Manual can opener

Personal Items and Documents

- **Medications:** Minimum 7-day supply, plus any necessary medical equipment

- **Glasses** or contact lens necessities

- **Important documents:** insurance policies, identification, bank account records, etc. in a waterproof, portable container

- **Personal hygiene items:** toothbrush, toothpaste, soap, feminine hygiene products, etc.

- **Copies of keys** to your house and car

For Families

- **Infant formula,** bottles, diapers, wipes, diaper rash cream

- Children's medications

- **Pet food** and extra water for your pet

- **Books, games, puzzles** or other activities for children

If You Must Evacuate

- **Sleeping bag** or warm blanket for each person

- **Change of clothes** and sturdy shoes for each person

- Emergency contact information for family or friends

Remember, these lists provide basic necessities for a hurricane survival kit. You should modify them to meet the specific needs of your family and pets. Consider needs like dietary restrictions, allergy requirements, and pet considerations. Also remember to update these supplies regularly - things like medications and food can expire, and needs can change from year to year.

Preparing for a hurricane can seem like a massive task, but having a comprehensive checklist can help ease the stress.

It's about ensuring that you have the essentials to remain safe and look after your loved ones during any storm that comes your way.

Appendix B: Evacuation Route Maps

Having an evacuation map at your fingertips can be the difference between escaping safely and being left stranded in the throes of a natural disaster. However, getting your hands on the correct routes isn't always easy, especially when you're scrambling at the last minute. Below, we complicate a bit of that process and bring you reliable evacuation routes that are applicable for those in the west coast of Florida.

Always remember, an evacuation route isn't as simple as getting from Point A to Point B. It requires an understanding of traffic management, anticipated congestion, and potential roadblocks caused by the hurricane. This is why relying on reputable sources for evacuation route information is critical.

West Coast of Florida Evacuation Routes

The following are significant evacuations routes that are most commonly used and suggested by local authorities in the event of a hurricane evacuation along the West Coast of Florida.

- **I-75:** Spanning the entire western length of Florida, this is a key highway that runs from south, beginning in Naples, and heads north toward Tampa, and then continues on to the Georgia border. This highway can be very busy, especially in times of evacuation, so keep up to date with local traffic reports.

- **US-41 (Tamiami Trail):** This is another major north-south artery that runs parallel to I-75. It starts in Miami, and hugs the Gulf Coast up through Tampa. This is a non-limited access highway, so expect numerous stoplights and slower speeds.

- **US-19:** This highway, which starts in Memphis, Florida, branches off from US-41 just north of Tampa and provides a northward route toward Georgia. Similar to US-41, this is non-limited access with traffic lights, and thus traffic is typically slower.

Understanding the Map

The evacuation route map specifically designed for the residents of West Florida takes into account the residential zones in hurricane-prone areas. In these maps, different zones are typically color-coded based on their susceptibility to storm surge, from least (Zone A) to greatest (Zone E).

Whatever zone you're in, knowing your route is as important as knowing when to evacuate. Think it through, know the possible bottlenecks, road closures, construction areas, and have a backup plan. The more you know, the less likely it's gonna be a stumbling block in your path.

New Routes with Evacuation Map Update

Just as the weather patterns change, so do evacuation routes. These can change based on construction, changes in traffic patterns, or revised emergency plans. Stay informed by regularly checking with local authorities for the latest map updates.

Remember that an evacuation map doesn't just guide you out of a disaster area - it also helps first responders quickly aid those in need. They can identify pre-defined assembly points, relief distribution centers and routes for hospitals, among others.

Securing a hurricane evacuation map may seem like a minor detail - one that's easy to overlook when you're busy with the daily grind. But in the face of a storm, it becomes yet another piece in the puzzle that ensures your survival - and the faster are out of harm's way, the faster you can return to rebuilding your life.

In conclusion, always have a proper evacuation plan, keep your route map at an arm's reach, and keep it updated. Remember, there's no harm in being well-prepared, but there is certainly harm in being found lacking when the storm hits.

Appendix C: Important Contact Information

In the midst of hurricane chaos, it's mighty essential to have all the vital contact information handy. Below is a list of some key organizations, emergency services, and community resources that you might need before, during or after a hurricane. Be sure to keep this list within easy reach - you might not have internet access at the time you need this information the most.

Federal & State Services

1. National Weather Service (NWS): *Website* or Dial 1-202-647-3535

2. Federal Emergency Management Agency (FEMA): *Website* or Dial 1-800-621-FEMA

3. Florida Division of Emergency Management: *Website* or Dial 1-800-342-3557

Medical Emergencies

1. American Red Cross: *Website* or Dial 1-800-733-2767

2. Poison Control: Dial 1-800-222-1222

Utility Companies

If there's one thing a hurricane knows how to rock, it's your utilities. Jot down your local utilities phone numbers and their websites right here:

- Electricity Company

- Water and Sewage

- Natural Gas Company

- Phone/Internet Provider

Insurance Company

When the storm subsides, you're gonna need your insurance company on speed dial. Note down their contact details right here:

- Home/Property Insurance

- Auto Insurance

- Life and Health Insurance

Local Services

From emergency contacts to shelters and food banks, it's practical to have these on your radar:

1. Emergency Dial 911

2. Local Police Station

3. Local Fire Department

4. Local Hospital

5. Community Shelters

6. Food Banks

Stay alert and prepared, but remember that Floridians are a tough bunch. Together, we can weather any storm that the Atlantic throws our way. Keep this important contact information handy and stay safe.